ALL-AMERICAN
PALEO TABLE

CLASSIC HOMESTYLE COOKING FROM
A GRAIN-FREE PERSPECTIVE

Caroline Potter, NTP

creator of the blog colorfuleats.com and contributing author
of *The Ultimate Paleo Cookbook*

PAGE STREET
PUBLISHING CO.

PAGE STREET
PUBLISHING CO.

First published in 2015 by
Page Street Publishing Co.
27 Congress Street, Suite 105
Salem, MA 01970
www.pagestreetpublishing.com

Distributed by Macmillan; sales in Canada by The Canadian Manda Group.

21 20 19 18 17   1 2 3 4 5

ISBN-13: 978-1-62414-471-4
ISBN-10: 1-62414-471-3

Library of Congress Control Number: 2017942618

Cover and book design by Page Street Publishing Co.
Photography by Caroline Potter
Cover and Lifestyle Photography by Amber Schoniwitz
Watercolor Icons by Loren Burgess

Printed and bound in China

Page Street is proud to be a member of 1% for the Planet. Members donate one percent of their sales to one or more of the over 1,500 environmental and sustainability charities across the globe who participate in this program.

DEDICATION

To Stephen—Thank you for believing in my dreams, supporting and encouraging me in every aspect of life even when you are out to sea, and loving me more every day. This book is filled with so many memories of us cooking together that I will forever treasure.

To my Creator—Thank you for giving me a story to share, a second chance in life and the opportunity to choose joy daily.

Contents

From the Author

To me, life is celebrated at the table. It is the thought of gathering, making memories, laughing and filling our hearts with joy and mouths with delicious foods. It is in the quiet moments of sharing a cup of coffee with a friend, coming home after a long day to a warm meal or the endless preparation of a Thanksgiving feast. The table represents so much of life—daily life that is worth celebrating. Your table may be small and wooden or it may be grand; it may be a small breakfast nook or a picnic table outside. But this table is a place that brings comfort, where stories can be told, tears can be shed and life can truly be lived.

When I was diagnosed with Type 1 diabetes in college and started eating grain-free and Paleo, it was always the foods associated with memories and gatherings that I missed the most. It was the cold fall mornings tailgating before football games. It was Thanksgiving Day when I wanted to reach for a slice of apple pie. It is many Friday nights when all I really want to do is curl up on the couch with a box of pizza and watch movies with my husband.

With this new way of eating, I was scared beyond belief. I was scared I would never be able to enjoy normal-people foods again—I was scared I would never be able to cut a wedding cake with my husband (which you can find on page 94) or make cinnamon rolls with my future children on Christmas morning (page 222). Being diagnosed with an autoimmune disease was beyond difficult, and it's something I have to work at each day, but it has also brought me a huge sense of joy and passion for creating foods that are nourishing, comforting and happy. Looking back, I would never trade my diagnosis for anything, and I hope that I can continue to help others on their journey of health.

Well, with a husband from Texas serving in the U.S. Navy, a golden retriever by my side and my belief that hamburgers are their own food group, *All-American Paleo Table* was born! I wanted to re-create these classic American favorites—meals that are familiar to us and hopefully bring back lots of memories—from a healthy perspective, so that you can eat and feel great.

Many of these recipes are a collection of my childhood favorites, or dishes that you usually will find on my breakfast or dinner table. With the recipes, you will hear stories that make them come alive, and I hope that they remind you of your own memories as well!

Just because you are making a lifestyle change does not mean that you have to eliminate those recipes you hold dear, but it does require a few ingredient swaps, creativity and a whole lot of patience. My goal with this book was to re-create as many of those foods that we treasure as Americans, but using healthy ingredients.

As much as I hope that you savor every tasty bite, I hope you also savor the memories made by cooking and eating together!

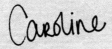

My Story—Finding Joy in Cooking and Health

Life in your 20s seems pretty grand—you feel powerful, youthful and energized! Dreams seem within your reach, and challenges appear to be conquerable. Then all of a sudden, college bliss turns into doctors' offices and waiting rooms. After six months of feeling sick all the time, countless tests of all forms, vague results and no answers as to what was wrong with me, I was finally diagnosed with an autoimmune disease, Type 1 diabetes.

When I came home from college for Christmas break, I lay on the couch for most of my vacation with little energy. I was constantly starving, but losing weight. Finally, one day while out to dinner with my family, I broke down in tears because my mouth was so dry, I could barely talk. I was experiencing dry mouth, one of the major symptoms of diabetes. Barely able even to walk up a flight of stairs, I checked myself into the emergency room and was given the news that I was diabetic.

To say this was a dark and difficult time in my life is an understatement—I was scared, confused and completely hopeless. I felt alone and had no clue how I would get through the rest of my life with this disease. The days that followed were miserable. Shortly after going on insulin, I gained 20 pounds within two weeks, nearly fainted multiple times every day and was completely embarrassed by my condition and looks. My legs, arms and stomach were black and blue from giving myself shots. Although I kept a smile on my face, emotionally I was struggling. The doctors just kept telling me I would be fine, that this was the way life would be from now on and to continue counting my carbs.

I have never been one to take no for an answer, and I knew there had to be a better way to live. Refusing just to be another statistic in the diabetic charts, I took matters into my own hands. I read and researched everything I could, from scientific studies to clinical trials and from nutrition books to old-fashioned homemade remedies. This is when I discovered a grain-free and Paleo way of eating.

Growing up in a home where my mother fed us very healthily—no sodas, candy or white bread—I was familiar with the basics of healthy eating, but never fully understood how it actually impacted everyday life. Through my research, I learned how sugars and carbohydrates affected my health at a cellular level, and, in turn, my condition.

I discovered that the more carbohydrates I consumed, the more insulin I would need. So I cut out all refined sugars, grains, gluten and most carbohydrates and instantly watched my insulin need decrease. For a while I ate strictly fats, proteins and leafy vegetables. I discovered that fats—butter, steak and eggs—which just so happened to be some of my favorite foods, were actually good for me! With the help of a nutritionist, endless encouragement from my family and following a very strict diet, I was slowly able to wean myself off insulin for about the next two years.

Currently, I am back on a very minimal, daily amount of insulin. My strict eating habits allow me to take such a small dosage that my doctors are amazed at how well I function. Yes, my body needs the insulin and I am beyond thankful that modern medicine can support my health, but to me that is not a reason to ditch a real food based lifestyle.

My health journey shaped my passions and gave me a love for cooking, teaching myself how to photograph and studying nutrition. In 2013, I became a Nutritional Therapy Practitioner (NTP), certified by the Nutritional Therapy Association, so I could better grasp the foundations of real food nutrition and understand how the body works on a cellular level—this all from the girl who barely passed biology in college!

This way of eating takes a bit of time and creativity, but now that I have seen firsthand how diet and nutrition allow me to feel so great, I could never go back to any other way of eating. Countless people have encouraged me never to give up on my health, and I hope these recipes bring cheer to your daily meal, no matter what your story or situation may be.

The Heart of the Table

"Food and cooking are among the richest subjects in the world. Every day of our lives, they preoccupy, delight and refresh us. Food is not just some fuel we need to get us going toward higher things. Cooking is not a drudgery we put up with in order to get the fuel delivered. Rather, each is a heart's astonishment. Both stop us dead in our tracks with wonder. Even more, they sit us down evening after evening, and in the company that forms around our table, they actually create our humanity." —Robert Farrar Capon

When I was growing up, family dinnertime was sacred in our house. As a child I never really understood this concept, but as I grew older and got married, I am thankful my mom and dad instilled this philosophy in me. When my husband was deployed a few years ago, this concept really hit me, because no matter how delicious or healthy the food I made was, it simply did not taste as good without someone to share it with. To me, food is more than just a means to fulfill hunger; it is a chance to create something from nothing, create something beautiful and sometimes, to create a disaster in the kitchen. But most important, food is a way that people of every walk of life can come together, sharing *in* life together.

Healthy eating can sometimes be a controversial topic, since everyone has their own opinions about what "healthy" means. But, rather than focusing on these differences, create a space that is welcoming, a table where all people can come to eat, be nourished and leave satisfied. For many celebrations, such as a birthday party or a Thanksgiving feast, food is usually the common language spoken. So how do you satisfy all tastes and preferences?

Create options for everyone so that no matter who comes to your table, they feel welcomed!

If you're having a backyard barbecue and grilling hamburgers, make the grain-free burger buns for you and whoever else wants them, but also provide some gluten-free or regular buns for those who wish to indulge. If it's taco night, have a gluten-free corn tortilla option for guests and make yourself a grain-free version. If you're attending a football or birthday party, offer to bring an appetizer along with a bag of sweet potato chips to your friend's house. That way you can share but also have something to eat so you don't feel excluded.

In the end it is about making people feel comfortable, about coming together to sit around the table and share, so don't get too hung up on perfection. As your loved ones and friends realize not only how great the food tastes but also how great they feel afterward, you might slowly convert people to a real food and Paleo way of eating. People may look at you differently at first, but soon they will start asking questions about your way of eating as they reach over to try your grain-free banana pancakes.

Start with the foods everyone loves—biscuits (page 40), smoked baby back ribs (page 98), fried chicken (page 128) or pepperoni pizza (page 180). Return to the kitchen to cook with your friends, children or significant other. Have family movie night or date night in your house rather than going out. Create memories by eating the food you made with your hands and your loved ones.

Making Your Paleo Table

Paleo is not just a word, diet or fad—it is an idea that helps define real food, food as it is commonly found in nature: food that has been around for centuries, before feedlots, before pasteurization, before chemicals and before genetic modifications.

I believe that the true purpose of the Paleo diet is embracing the foods that make you feel good and eliminating those that are processed and make you feel sick. Whatever those foods are for you, as long as you are eating real food and, of course, everything in moderation, I think that each individual needs to discover what foods work best for them. In the end, just eat real food—food that is from the earth, food that makes you feel good and food that puts a smile on your face.

So many times I see people become obsessed on whether something is Paleo or not. My biggest encouragement to you is to focus on eating real food—foods that make you thrive—and not get too consumed with every tiny detail. Keep the big picture in focus—this is a lifestyle, not a diet, a lifestyle that brings health, joy and freedom!

Foods to Avoid

A good rule of thumb: If you can't pronounce it, it probably isn't real food.

GRAINS

 » Wheat

 » Corn

 » Oats

 » Barley

 » Rye

 » Cereals or pastas

REFINED SUGARS

 » Agave syrup

 » Cane sugar

 » Sugar-free or calorie-free sweeteners

 » Artificial sweeteners

PROCESSED FOODS

 » Soy products

 » Low-fat, processed or pasteurized dairy

 » Hydrogenated or refined oils

Foods to Eat

A good rule of thumb: If it is fresh and perishable, it is probably a real food.

QUALITY ANIMAL PRODUCTS

 » Grass-fed and pasture-raised meats

 » Fresh, wild-caught fish

 » Eggs (organic or pasture-raised are best)

 » Raw or grass-fed dairy (good quality in moderation, if not allergic or sensitive)

FULL-FAT, UNREFINED OILS AND FATS

 » Olive, coconut and sesame oil

 » Avocados

 » Duck, bacon fat, tallow or other rendered animal lard

 » Grass-fed butter and ghee

OTHER FOODS

 » Fresh, seasonal fruits and vegetables

 » Fermented foods

 » Nuts and seeds

My take on dairy…that is, good-quality dairy!

I'll be honest—I absolutely love my grass-fed butter, cheeses of all flavors and spoonfuls of heavy whipping cream! However, there are different kinds of dairy—I am not talking about processed cheese that looks like plastic or the kind that can be squeezed out of a can, I am talking about real, full-fat dairy from healthy and humanely raised animals.

Dairy, as it occurs in nature, from cows, sheep or goats, comes from animals roaming in the pasture and munching on grasses. It's full fat and a beautiful creamy white color, not that bluish, let's-remove-all-the-fat-and-flavor kind you find on most grocery store shelves. And most important, this dairy contains important vitamins and nutrients that provide your body with energy and nourishment.

For example, grass-fed butter is rich in CLA, conjugated linoleic acid, a fatty acid that boosts your metabolism and can help support weight loss, as well as vitamin K, a fat-soluble vitamin that actually protects your heart and arteries. Raw, grass-fed dairy provides beneficial bacteria that is good for the digestive and immune systems as well as vitamins A and D, which are common deficiencies in the standard American diet.

The problem with conventional dairy is that the process of pasteurization destroys the countless nutrients found in raw dairy. For example lactase, the enzyme that enables us to digest the sugar lactose, is destroyed during pasteurization but remains present in raw dairy. So yes, pasteurized milk can make you feel horribly sick, myself included.

No, cavemen did not eat dairy any more than they ate a perfectly grilled steak, breakfast tacos, coconut milk lattes or strawberries in the middle of winter. But that's missing the point of choosing to eat real food, food as it is commonly found in nature and food that makes you feel great! In the end, a Paleo or real food diet, is about having a better relationship with our food, learning where our food came from, and seeing how this lifestyle can bring so much joy and health back into our daily meals.

I happen to do very well with grass-fed raw cheeses and whipped cream added to desserts or the occasional cappuccino. That said, if you are allergic to dairy or working through a specific health issue, by all means please don't eat it!

Please note: For recipes not marked "dairy free" that means that removing the dairy option from the ingredients will completely change the recipe. Some recipes include dairy as optional or simply as a garnish. Recipes that I can only recommend using butter or ghee are not marked "dairy free" because although ghee does not contain casein or lactose, which some people have difficulty digesting, it is still made from dairy products.

A Morning Rise

Daily Rituals for Breakfast, Brunch and Coffee Dates

Breakfast is my favorite meal of the day and the most important one at that. These recipes are staples to keep on hand and will add some cheer to your morning routine. If you are like me and fall asleep dreaming of what to make for breakfast, this chapter is for you!

CRUNCHY CINNAMON TOAST SQUARES

Nut Free, Dairy Free

Based on the classic childhood favorite, this cereal has been transformed into a healthy version that's also nut free, so those with allergies can enjoy it too! Like any of my sweet treats, keep in mind that this cereal may not be as sweet as the ones you find on grocery store shelves. It has a bit of crunch to it and is great topped with your milk of choice or even eaten by the handful.

MAKES ABOUT 3 CUPS (65 G) OF CEREAL

½ cup (70 g) creamy sunflower seed butter

3 tbsp (26 g) maple sugar

1 tbsp (15 ml) coconut oil

1 tbsp (6 g) coconut flour

1 tbsp (9 g) arrowroot flour

1 egg

2 tsp (5 g) ground cinnamon

1 tsp (5 ml) vanilla extract

Maple Cinnamon Sprinkles

1 tbsp (9 g) maple sugar

½ tsp ground cinnamon

Preheat the oven to 275°F (135°C). Line a baking sheet with parchment paper and set aside. Arrange the oven rack to the middle position.

Use a hand mixer to mix all the cereal ingredients together until a smooth and slightly thick ball of batter forms. Scrape down the sides of the bowl and briefly blend again.

Place the batter on the parchment paper, using a spatula to smooth out into a very thin shape about 12 by 10 inches (25.5 by 30.5 cm). You want to spread this out as thin as possible without creating any holes. Be patient because this process is key to the texture.

Mix together the maple cinnamon sprinkle ingredients and sprinkle on top of the cereal dough.

Bake for 48 to 50 minutes, watching carefully at the end so that it does not burn, but keep in mind that the cereal hardens once cool. Remove from the oven and cool completely, allowing the cereal to crisp. Once it is cool, break into small, bite-size pieces.

Serve with yogurt or milk of choice, or even by the handful.

This & That

Many sunflower seed butters, even some at the health food store, contain added oils, sugars and other bad ingredients. Make sure to choose a butter made entirely of ground sunflower seeds.

MEXICAN CHORIZO SAUSAGE

Nut Free, Dairy Free, No Added Sugar

Sausage and fried eggs is my all-time favorite breakfast, and this chorizo sausage will take your breakfast to another level. It's spicy, oh-so-delicious and a great addition to tacos, nachos or even salads.

MAKES 10 ROUND BREAKFAST-SIZE SAUSAGE PATTIES

1 tbsp (9 g) ancho chili powder

2½ tsp (13 g) salt

2 tsp (6 g) ground cumin

1½ tsp (4 g) paprika

1 tsp (3 g) black pepper

¾ tsp cayenne pepper

½ tsp smoked paprika

¼ tsp ground cinnamon

2 lbs (910 g) ground pork

2 tbsp (30 ml) apple cider vinegar

3 large cloves garlic, crushed

In a small prep bowl, add all the dried spices, mixing together to create the spice blend.

Add the ground pork to a large mixing bowl. Sprinkle about ⅓ of the spice blend, 1 tablespoon (15 ml) of the apple cider vinegar and one of the crushed garlic gloves over the ground pork. Use your hands to lightly massage the spices into the meat; this does not need to be fully mixed. Continue this process until all the spice blend, apple cider vinegar and garlic are used and the meat is evenly mixed.

Wrap the meat tightly in plastic wrap and refrigerate for 24 hours. You can also divide the meat in half, saving it for other recipes or even freezing it for later. (If you do freeze the sausage, make sure you allow it to marinate for the complete time first before freezing.)

When you are ready to cook your sausage, warm a skillet to medium heat. Grab a handful of the meat and use your hands to shape into flat round sausage patties.

Sear the sausage for 4 to 5 minutes, flip to the other side and continue cooking for an additional 4 to 5 minutes or until the meat is thoroughly cooked.

Serve with eggs or even make the sausage patties into breakfast sandwiches using Sandwich Rolls (page 150).

This & That
I usually double the recipe, freezing some of the raw meat then using it to make breakfast tacos (page 28) or Cheddar Chorizo Dip (page 160).

NUT-FREE BANANA BREAD WAFFLES

Nut Free, Dairy Free, No Added Sugar

Breakfasts filled with hot coffee and relaxing mornings around the table are a favorite in our house. Sweetened with real bananas and a slight hint of spice, these light and fluffy waffles are a Saturday morning favorite, with a side of bacon of course! I often double the batch to keep extras on hand for a quick weekday-morning breakfast. Personally, I try to keep my sugars to a minimum, and the bananas make these waffles sweet enough, so I usually just top mine with a pat of butter and scoop of whipped cream.

MAKES 6 ROUND WAFFLES

1½ cups (345 g) mashed yellow bananas* (about 4 medium bananas)

4 eggs, separated

2 egg whites

4 tbsp (58 g) butter or ghee**, melted

1 tsp (5 ml) vanilla extract

½ cup (50 g) coconut flour, sifted

2 tbsp (17 g) arrowroot flour

1½ tsp (4 g) ground cinnamon

½ tsp baking soda

¼ tsp baking powder

¼ tsp ground nutmeg

Coconut oil, for greasing the waffle iron

You want the bananas to be ripe and yellow but not overly ripe or completely brown.

**Use coconut oil for strict dairy free.*

Preheat the waffle iron to medium heat.

On a plate, mash the bananas with a fork until completely smooth, measure the correct amount and then place in a mixing bowl.

Separate the eggs, adding the yolks to the banana mixture and the whites, plus two additional whites, into a separate bowl, for a total of six egg whites.

Using a hand mixer, whip the egg whites until slightly stiff, foamy peaks begin to form, and set aside.

Add the melted butter and vanilla extract to the banana mixture and mix. Next sift in all remaining dry ingredients. Blend with a hand mixer until smooth. Scrape down the sides and bottom of the bowl before briefly blending again.

Gently fold the egg whites into the banana batter so that the mixture is thoroughly mixed but not flattened.

Just as you are about to cook, generously brush the waffle iron with coconut oil.

Use a large spoon to drop batter into the center of the waffle iron. Do not fill completely because the batter will spread out. Cook until the waffle iron signals the waffles are finished.

Repeat with the remaining batter until all waffles are made.

Serve hot with Blackberry Skillet Jam (pg 32), melted butter or maple syrup.

This & That

I have found that when working with coconut flour and bananas, a firm yellow banana works best, otherwise your waffles will end up slightly soggy. So if you are impatient, like me, waiting for bananas to ripen, this recipe is for you!

These waffles store fabulously in the fridge or freezer. Simply place cooled waffles between layers of parchment paper in an airtight container and use for a quick breakfast throughout the week.

ROSEMARY BACON FRIED EGGS

Nut Free, Dairy Free, No Added Sugar

Fried eggs are one of my favorite breakfasts, but this version dresses up
this morning meal with a bit of bacon and fresh rosemary.

SERVES 1

2 slices bacon

½ tsp fresh rosemary, chopped

2 eggs

Salt and pepper to taste

Warm a small skillet to medium heat. Cut the bacon into small pieces.

Sauté the bacon and fresh rosemary for about 2 minutes or until the bacon bits are browned and slightly crispy.

Divide the bacon in half and arrange into two small circles in the skillet. Crack each egg in the middle of the bacon crumbles. Allow the edges to slightly sizzle and become crispy for about 30 seconds, then turn the heat down to low.

Cook the eggs until the whites are mostly set, then carefully flip to the other side and cook to desired preference. Season with salt and pepper to taste.

Plate and serve with a slice of toasted Nut-Free Sandwich Bread (page 30) or Morning Butter Biscuits (page 40).

This & That

While cooking your bacon, it should give off enough grease to fry the eggs, but if not, simply add a drizzle of olive oil to the pan to make sure the eggs don't stick.

STRAWBERRY CHOCOLATE GRANOLA

Dairy Free

Making granola grain-free is quite simple, and this recipe is a staple in our house for quick breakfasts, snacks or treats that are delicious but full of nutrients as well. Cacao nibs are unsweetened chocolate bits that provide a rich, slightly smoky contrast to the sweet strawberries. Serve with your milk or yogurt of choice or just nibble on as a snack.

MAKES BETWEEN 3 AND 4 CUPS (180 AND 270 GRAMS)

½ cup (119 ml) fresh strawberry puree

1½ cups (256 g) raw almonds

1½ cups (204 g) raw macadamia nuts

¼ cup (34 g) golden flaxseed, finely ground

3 tbsp (44 ml) coconut oil

1 tbsp (15 ml) raw honey

¾ cup (96 g) cacao nibs

1 oz (28 g) freeze-dried strawberries

Preheat the oven to 300°F (148°C) and arrange the baking rack in the middle of the oven. Line a baking sheet with parchment paper.

To make the fruit puree, blend fresh strawberries in a food processor. Remove and measure out ½ cup (119 ml) puree.

In the food processor, pulse nuts, flaxseed, oil and honey until crumbly, being careful not to overblend into nut butter. Add in cacao nibs and fruit puree. Pulse several times. Use a spatula to fold in the dried strawberries.

Scoop onto the baking sheet and spread evenly, creating a thin, even layer. Bake for 28 to 32 minutes or until golden brown, slightly crunchy and fragrant.

Allow the granola to cool completely before breaking into granola-like pieces.

Serve with yogurt or milk and top with fresh berries.

Store any remaining granola in an airtight container in the refrigerator or cool location for 7-10 days.

CHORIZO AND CRISPY POTATO BREAKFAST TACOS

Nut Free, Dairy Free, No Added Sugar

Nothing quite says American like good old-fashioned breakfast potatoes. I love this dish so much
that I often make it into a hearty breakfast hash when I don't have tortillas on hand. The process of searing
the potatoes in duck fat then finishing them off in the oven gives these breakfast potatoes the perfect crispy
outsides and soft centers. These tacos are a nutricious combination of healthy fats, protein
and carbohydrates to keep you satisfied all morning long!

MAKES 4 BREAKFAST TACOS

2 tbsp (17 g) duck fat

1 medium russet potato

½ tsp sea salt

¼ tsp garlic powder

¼ recipe or ½ lb (680 g) Mexican
Chorizo Sausage (page 20)

4 eggs

2 tbsp (30 ml) full-fat unsweetend
coconut milk or grass-fed heavy cream

4 Soft Plantain Tortillas (page 84),
warmed

Avocado slices, to garnish

Preheat the oven to 400°F (204°C) and warm a large skillet to medium heat, melting
the duck fat in the pan.

Cut the potato into small cubes, no larger than ½-inch (1.3-cm) thick squares. Add
the potatoes to the skillet to sear and cook for 10 minutes, stirring occasionally so
they don't stick to the bottom.

Transfer the potatoes and all oil in the pan to a rimmed baking sheet, tossing them
together with the salt and garlic powder. Roast for 15 to 20 minutes, stirring halfway
through, or until the potatoes are tender and golden brown.

While the potatoes are roasting, prepare your chorizo sausage in the skillet,
browning and crumbling for about 5 minutes or until it is fully cooked. Remove the
sausage from the pan with a slotted spoon and set aside.

Whisk together the eggs and milk until smooth. Scramble the eggs in the pan to your
desired preference with the leftover grease, adding more duck fat if necessary.

Assemble the tacos by dividing the potatoes, chorizo and eggs among the tortillas.

Garnish with avocado slices.

This & That
Classic breakfast potatoes are made with white russet potatoes, which
I enjoy eating occasionally, especially when fried in duck fat. You can
substitute sweet potatoes, and it will still be delicious!

NUT-FREE SANDWICH BREAD

Nut Free, No Added Sugar

This new version of sandwich bread is taken from my original grain- and nut-free sandwich bread on my blog, Colorful Eats, but I worked to improve the taste and texture. Keep in mind that this version is slightly higher in starchy carbohydrates than the original one, but still nut free. It has a very soft center and crusty outside, perfect for filling with your favorite sandwich toppings or just toasting with a pat of butter.

MAKES ONE BREAD LOAF

Coconut oil

6 tbsp (86 g) butter or ghee, melted

½ cup (50 g) coconut flour, sifted

¼ cup (34 g) sweet potato starch* or potato starch

¼ cup (34 g) arrowroot flour

2 tbsp (18 g) psyllium husk powder

1 tsp (5 g) baking soda

½ tsp baking powder

¼ tsp salt

4 whole eggs

2 tbsp (30 ml) full-fat, unsweetened coconut milk

1 tbsp (15 ml) apple cider vinegar

4 egg whites

Sweet potato starch is a white starchy flour, unlike sweet potato flour, which is orange in color and bakes very differently. See explanation page 242.

Preheat the oven to 350°F (176°C), arranging the baking rack to the middle position. Line an 8½ by 4½ inch (22 by 12 cm) loaf pan with parchment paper lengthwise and brush the outer ends lightly with coconut oil. Tear off a piece of foil slightly larger than the loaf pan and set it aside for later.

Melt the butter in a separate small saucepan and set aside.

In a mixing bowl, sift together all the dry ingredients and set aside. Add in the melted butter, whole eggs and coconut milk to the bowl with the flour. Blend until smooth, scraping down the sides and bottom of the bowl. Lastly, add the apple cider vinegar and blend again. (At this point you want to work quickly to get your bread into the oven because the vinegar, eggs and baking soda have begun their reaction.)

Add the egg whites to a mixing bowl and use a hand mixer to whip until soft, foamy peaks begin to form.

Next, add the whipped egg whites to the batter and blend on low until the mixture is fully mixed. It is okay that the egg whites fall a bit, but your bread batter should still be pretty light and foamy.

Pour the batter into the prepared loaf pan, gently smoothing out the top with a spatula.

Place the piece of foil over the top, lightly tenting and allowing room for the bread to rise.

Place in the oven and bake for a total of 70 minutes, removing the foil halfway through.

Remove the bread from the oven and set on a cooling rack for 15 minutes before lifting up the edges of the parchment paper to remove from the pan. Allow it to cool completely.

Slice, butter and enjoy!

Store any extra bread in the refrigerator, wrapped tightly to keep it from drying out, and toast as needed.

This & That

I recommend sifting your coconut flour before measuring and then sifting again as you add the dry ingredients to the batter. Exact measurements are very important.

This bread does rise nicely, but keep in mind it is a smaller loaf, about 2½ inches (6.3 cm) tall.

BLACKBERRY SKILLET JAM

Nut Free, Dairy Free

When fresh blackberries are crushed and turned into jam, something extraordinary happens. Add a scoop to Skillet Peach Cobbler (page 106), serve over warm biscuits (page 40) or eat by the spoonful straight from the skillet.

MAKES ABOUT 2 CUPS (475 ML) OF JAM

1 lb (454 g) fresh blackberries

¼ cup (59 ml) water

4-6 tbsp (60-90 ml) raw honey, depending on desired sweetness*

2 tsp (10 ml) fresh squeezed lemon juice

1½ tsp (5 g) grass-fed gelatin

Warm a skillet to medium-low heat. Add the blackberries and water and heat for 10 minutes.

Next, use the back of a large wooden spoon to crush the berries, releasing their juice.

Stir in the honey, lemon juice and gelatin. Heat for an additional 10 minutes, allowing the jam to slightly simmer.

Remove the skillet from the heat and set aside to cool for 15 minutes before transferring to an airtight container and placing in the refrigerator. Cool the jam for 4 hours, allowing it to thicken.

Spread on warm biscuits, sandwich bread or even add a scoop to vanilla ice cream!

This & That

*I prefer a tarter jam with less sweetener, so I usually use 4 tablespoons (60 ml) of honey to sweeten. Keep in mind that blackberries vary in their sweetness depending on the season and how fresh they are, so adjust the amount of honey according to your tastes.

HAZELNUT VANILLA BEAN MILK OR COFFEE CREAMER

Dairy Free, No Added Sugar

Hazelnuts have a nutty yet mild flavor that pairs beautifully with your morning cup of coffee!
They are quite high in vitamin E, which acts as an antioxidant, helping cleanse your body as well as
decreasing inflammation. Vitamin E specifically helps the health and integrity of the cell membrane, which is
of primary importance to overall health. You can also use this as a dairy-free milk alternative
by adding it to smoothies, milkshakes or with granola.

YIELDS ABOUT 3½ CUPS (828 ML) MILK

1 cup (170 g) raw hazelnuts

4 cups (947 ml) water, divided

¼ tsp salt

1 cup (237 ml) full-fat, unsweetend coconut milk

1 vanilla bean, sliced open and seeds removed

Place the hazelnuts in a glass bowl and add 2 cups (475 ml) of water and salt. Cover the bowl and set aside to soak for 8 to 12 hours at room temperature.

Strain and rinse the hazelnuts. Add the nuts and remaining 2 cups (475 ml) of water to a high-speed blender. Blend for about 2 minutes or until smooth and foamy. Strain the milk through a nut bag or fine mesh strainer and discard the hazelnut pulp.

Add the strained hazelnut milk back into the blender along with the salt, coconut milk and vanilla bean. Blend briefly.

Store the milk in an airtight glass jar in the refrigerator for up to 4 days.

HAWAIIAN AÇAÍ BOWLS

Nut Free, Dairy Free, No Added Sugar

One of my favorite parts of being stationed at Pearl Harbor, Hawaii, is being able to experience new and very unique tropical foods. These tropical fruit bowls are a staple here in Hawaii; however most bowls you find at restaurants or beachside food trucks are loaded with sugar and topped with sugar- and grain-filled granola. Good news—they are simple to make in your own kitchen, and the topping ideas are endless!

SERVES 2

2 (3.5 oz [100g]) packets unsweetened, frozen açaí berry

½ banana, sliced and frozen

½ cup (68 g) frozen strawberries

¼ cup (34 g) frozen blueberries

1 cup (237 ml) full-fat, unsweetened coconut milk

1 tsp (3 g) grass-fed gelatin

Topping Ideas
Fresh banana, mango, papaya or kiwi slices

Macadamia nuts

Toasted coconut flakes

Cacao nibs

Drizzle of raw honey

Spoonful of Strawberry Chocolate Granola (page 26)

Set the frozen açaí on the counter to thaw for 10 minutes.

Next, place the açaí, banana, strawberries, blueberries, coconut milk and gelatin in a blender. Blend on high until smooth.

Serve over yogurt or as a smoothie with your favorite toppings.

This & That
Unsweetened açaí packets are a bit more difficult to find than the sweetened version, however most health food stores carry them.

A Farmer's Breakfast

Classic Home Cooking for a Morning Meal

There is nothing quite like a lazy morning and a big breakfast spread! I absolutely love pouring a hot cup of coffee and taking a relaxing morning to prepare a scrumptious breakfast. These recipes take a bit more time to prepare, but are perfect for weekends with your family or when having friends over for brunch. So pull out the cast iron skillets, because comfort food is about to be cooking in your kitchen!

MORNING BUTTER BISCUITS

Dairy Free

These biscuits are my absolute favorite baked creation. Cashews have a light, mellow flavor, so you will
hardly notice that the biscuits are made with nuts and that they are very low in carbohydrates—a great staple
to keep in the kitchen. These are slightly denser than their gluten-filled predecessors, but are so buttery and
delicious that you will probably want to eat more than one—yes, I can say that with experience! I like to
freeze any extras to keep on hand for a snack or bit of comfort food because if you are
anything like me, you will probably be craving these!

MAKES 8 BISCUITS

6 tbsp (86 g) butter*

3 cups (435 g) raw cashew pieces

3 tbsp (18 g) coconut flour

1 tsp (3 g) grass-fed gelatin

1 tsp (4.5 g) baking soda

½ tsp baking powder

¼ tsp salt

1 tbsp (15 ml) raw honey

2 eggs

2 tsp (10 ml) apple cider vinegar

Coconut oil for greasing hands

*Palm shortening can be used for strictly
dairy-free, but I prefer them best using
butter.*

Slice butter into small cubes and set aside to soften for 15 minutes.

Preheat the oven to 350°F (176°C), adjusting the rack to the bottom portion of the
oven. Line a baking sheet with parchment paper.

Add the cashew pieces to the bowl of a food processor and blend for about 30 seconds
or until a smooth nut flour begins to form. Be careful not to turn into nut butter.

Next, add the flour, gelatin, baking soda, baking powder and salt, pulsing several
times to incorporate.

Finally, add the softened butter, honey, eggs and vinegar and briefly blend for about
10 seconds or until the dough starts to form.

Lightly grease your hands with coconut oil. Pinch off a small handful of dough and
shape into biscuits, using your fingers to form a smooth top and round shape. Place
on the baking sheet about 3 inches (7.6 cm) apart, because these biscuits do expand
a bit. Repeat the process to form all the biscuits. If your dough becomes too sticky,
wash and lightly re-oil your hands.

Bake for 16 to 18 minutes, then remove from the oven and allow the biscuits to cool
on the baking sheet for 5 minutes, so they firm up.

Serve warm with butter, Blackberry Skillet Jam (page 32) or White Sausage Gravy
(page 46).

This & That

I decided to use cashew pieces as opposed to whole cashews; they're
generally more cost effective. You can use whole cashews if that is what you
have. Just use about 15 ounces (425 g).

STEAK AND EGG BREAKFAST FRIES

Nut Free, Dairy Free, No Added Sugar

In our house, we love eating steak and eggs for breakfast so much that we often make extras of Stephen's
Fire–Grilled Filet Mignon (page 70) to enjoy the next morning, which was how this dish was originally created!
It does take a few steps to prepare, but each component comes together to create a dreamy flavor and texture
with each bite. So pour yourself a cup of coffee and enjoy this brunch-style meal in the comfort of your home.

SERVES 2

1 (8 oz [227 g]) filet mignon steak

¼ cup (60 ml) Smoky Hollandaise Sauce
(page 56), for serving

2 russet potatoes

¼ cup (34 g) duck fat

2 tsp (6 g) Cajun Seasoning (page 140)

½ small red onion, thinly sliced

Salt and black pepper to taste

2 poached eggs with runny yolks

½ tsp white vinegar

This & That

Sweet potatoes can easily be
substituted for regular potatoes,
and their sweetness pairs nicely
with the smoky undertones of
this dish.

You can easily double or triple
the recipe, depending on how
many people you are serving.

Preheat the oven to 400°F (204°C) and warm a large skillet to medium heat. Line
a baking sheet with parchment paper. Set the steak on the counter to reach room
temperature. If not already prepared, start preparing the hollandaise sauce.

Slice the potatoes into about 1-inch (2.5-cm)-thick fries, just a little thicker than regular fries.

Add 2 tablespoons (30 ml) of the duck fat to the warm skillet along with the fries,
making sure none are piled on top of each other. Sear the fries for 10 minutes,
rotating occasionally.

Place the fries along with any remaining oil on the baking sheet, sprinkling with the
Cajun seasoning. Bake the fries in the oven for 15 to 20 minutes or until the fries start
to turn golden brown and crispy.

Add another tablespoon (15 ml) of duck fat to the pan. Sauté the onions for 15 minutes
or until soft. Remove and set aside.

Next, season the steak with salt and pepper. Add the last remaining tablespoon (15 ml)
of duck fat to the hot skillet. Sear the steak for 4 to 4½ minutes, depending on its
size and thickness, flip to the other side and continue cooking for 4 to 4½ additional
minutes, being careful not to overcook the filet.

While the steak is cooking, prepare the poached eggs by bringing 2 inches (5 cm)
of water to a gently bubbling simmer (not a rolling boil). Add a pinch of salt and
the vinegar to the pan. Crack a fresh egg into a small bowl. Just as you are about to
drop the egg into the water, use a spoon to stir the water in the same direction for 10
seconds, then carefully drop the egg into the water. For a soft poach with runny yolks,
poach for 2 to 2½ minutes, however timing will vary depending on your cooking
environment. Remove the egg with a slotted spoon to drain out any excess water and
repeat the process with each additional egg.

Now, it is time to assemble. Add a scoop of fries to each plate, then top with caramelized
onions, slices of steak, a poached egg and a generous drizzle of hollandaise sauce.

BANANA CHOCOLATE CHIP GRIDDLE CAKES

Dairy Free, No Added Sugar

These banana pancakes are so simple that you can teach anyone, even your kids, how to make them.
Chestnut flour has a slight spice flavor, so it pairs well with the sweet bananas. I make mine without chocolate
chips for a sugar-free option, but go ahead and drop in some chocolate if you like!

MAKES ABOUT 16 MEDIUM-SIZE PANCAKES

1 cup (230 g) mashed banana (about 2 large bananas)

1 cup (110 g) chestnut flour, sifted

4 eggs

1 tsp (5 ml) vanilla extract

¼ tsp baking soda

1 tbsp (15 g) butter or coconut oil, for greasing griddle

⅓ cup (60 g) chocolate chips, optional

Warm a griddle or large skillet to medium heat.

Use a fork to mash the bananas, measuring out the needed amount. In a mixing bowl, combine all the ingredients, except for the butter and chocolate chips, using a hand mixer to form a smooth batter.

Melt a pat of butter on the griddle and drop a spoonful of batter onto the griddle. The edges should sizzle slightly if the griddle is the right heat. Sprinkle a few chocolate chips, if using, on top. After about 1 to 1½ minutes, or until the edges are mostly set, carefully flip to the other side, cooking for about 30 more seconds.

Repeat until all the batter has been used.

Serve griddle cakes warm with butter, maple syrup or whipped cream.

This & That

You can double the batch and freeze extras for a quick breakfast option—simply cool completely and freeze between layers of parchment paper in an airtight container.

I like to make a warm maple syrup by melting together 2 tablespoons (30 g) butter, 2 tablespoons (30 ml) water and ½ cup (120 ml) maple syrup.

WHITE SAUSAGE GRAVY WITH BISCUITS

Dairy Free, No Added Sugar

After many requests from my husband for a healthy version of sausage gravy and biscuits on weekend mornings, I created this dish! I have never been a big gravy fan, but this hearty gravy filled with savory sausage is now one of my favorites. Pour a spoonful over warm Morning Butter Biscuits (page 40).

SERVES 4

1 lb (454 g) pork breakfast sausage, preferably sugar-free

1½ tbsp (6 g) arrowroot powder

2 tsp (4 g) coconut flour

1 tsp (5 g) fresh sage, finely chopped

½ tsp salt

¼–½ tsp fresh cracked black pepper, to taste

2 cups (473 ml) full-fat, unsweetened coconut milk

4 Morning Butter Biscuits (page 40), warmed

Warm a skillet to medium heat for at least 5 minutes, allowing it to completely heat up. Add the sausage to the hot skillet, browning and crumbling it into small pieces for about 5 minutes or until completely cooked. Use a slotted spoon to remove the sausage crumbles and set aside. Keep 1 tablespoon (15 ml) of the sausage grease in the pan and discard the rest.

Reduce the pan heat to low. Sprinkle the arrowroot and coconut flour evenly throughout the pan, stirring to avoid creating any clumps. Add the sage, salt and pepper and stir again, scraping down any brown sausage bits that stick to the bottom of the pan. This should be a pretty thick mixture.

Slowly pour in the milk, about ⅓ cup (80 ml) at a time, stirring and allowing the gravy to thicken before adding more milk. Once you have added all the milk, continue stirring together until a smooth gravy begins to form and thicken. Slowly stir for about a minute before mixing in the sausage crumbles.

Serve a generous spoonful over warm Morning Butter Biscuits.

This & That

Many sausages contain added preservatives, sugars and even gluten, so I usually look for a sugar-free pork breakfast sausage and always double-check the ingredients. For this dish, I like the sausage to have a bit of sage and black pepper because they add amazing flavor.

If you cannot have nuts in the biscuits, simply serve this over roasted sweet potatoes or crispy breakfast potatoes (page 28)!

CINNAMON SWIRL COFFEE CRUMB CAKE

Sometimes your cup of coffee needs a little sweet treat! Cashews give this cake a light appeal,
and if you can't find cashew flour you can easily make it yourself. This coffee cake is perfect to bring to
brunch or serve when guests are over. It is something everyone will enjoy.

MAKES ONE 8 BY 8-INCH (20 BY 20-CM) SQUARE CAKE

Coconut oil, for greasing cake pan

Cinnamon Swirl

3 tbsp (43 g) butter or ghee

1½ tbsp (13 g) maple sugar

1 tbsp (8 g) ground cinnamon

¼ tsp ground nutmeg

Crumb Topping

½ cup (60 g) pecans

2 tbsp (29 g) butter or ghee, softened

1 tbsp (9 g) maple sugar

1 tsp (3 g) ground cinnamon

Cake Ingredients

2 cups (193 g) cashew flour

¼ cup (24 g) coconut flour

¼ cup (50 g) coconut sugar

2 tbsp (17 g) maple sugar*

½ tsp baking soda

6 tbsp (86 g) butter or ghee, melted

4 eggs

1 tsp (5 ml) vanilla extract

*I often omit this extra maple sugar for
myself to keep the recipe a little less
sweet. Either way, it's a great recipe.

Preheat the oven to 350°F (176°C). Brush all sides and the bottom of an 8 by 8 inch (20.3 by 20.3 cm) baking pan with coconut oil and set aside.

In a small saucepan, melt together all cinnamon swirl ingredients and set aside for later.

In the bowl of a food processor, add all crumb topping ingredients, pulsing several times to a crumb-like consistency.

To make the cake batter, sift together all the dry ingredients. In a separate bowl, blend the melted butter, eggs and vanilla until slightly frothy. Add in the dry ingredients and blend to a smooth batter. Scrape down the sides and bottom of the bowl and briefly blend again.

Pour the coffee cake batter into the prepared baking dish. Next, slowly drizzle the cinnamon swirl butter around the pan, using a toothpick to swirl the butter into the cake batter. Finally, sprinkle on the crumb topping, evenly covering the top of the cake.

Now it's time to bake. Place the coffee cake on the middle oven rack and bake for 21 to 23 minutes. Allow cake to cool for 10 minutes before slicing and serving.

This & That

You can make your own cashew flour easily by grinding cashew pieces in a food processor. Just be sure to measure out the correct amount of flour. Trader Joe's is the best place to find packaged cashew flour.

COWBOY SKILLET HASH

Nut Free, Dairy Free, No Added Sugar

Breakfast hash is a flavorful and filling option to serve to guests or to keep on hand for a simple weekday breakfast because you can never go wrong with the cobination of sweet potatoes, bacon and eggs for some healthy comfort food. Jalapeños add a bit of heat, but hash options are endless, so feel free to play around with the vegetable combinations to suit your flavor preference.

SERVES 4

½ lb (227 g) bacon

2 medium-size sweet potatoes

¼ cup (45 g) bacon grease

½ tsp salt

½ tsp garlic powder

½ tsp smoked paprika

¼ tsp black pepper

1 sweet red bell pepper, minced

½ jalapeño pepper, seeds removed and minced*

2 green onions, thinly sliced

Poached or scrambled eggs to serve

*When removing the seeds and chopping, be sure to wear gloves to avoid any tearful situations.

Preheat oven to 400°F (204°C) and warm a large skillet to medium-low heat. Cook the bacon slices in the skillet until they are brown and crispy on both sides. Remove the bacon and set aside, keeping the grease in the pan.

While the bacon is cooking, slice the sweet potatoes into thin rounds, about ¼-inch thick, or as thin as you can make them.

Turn up the skillet heat to medium and cook the sweet potatoes in the bacon grease for 10 minutes, flipping halfway through. Add extra grease if necessary to prevent the potatoes from sticking to the pan. You may need to sear them in batches depending on the size of your pan, because overcrowding will not give you a great texture.

Transfer the sweet potatoes to a rimmed baking sheet along with the bacon grease from the pan. Toss together with the salt, garlic powder, paprika and pepper and place in the oven. Roast for 15 to 20 minutes or until tender and slightly crispy.

While the potatoes are cooking, sauté the peppers and onions for 10 minutes or until soft. Crumble the bacon and stir it into the pan at the end.

While everything is finishing cooking, prepare the eggs your favorite way—for this dish I prefer poached (instructions on page 42) or scrambled.

Remove the roasted sweet potatoes from the oven and mix together with the vegetables and bacon. Plate and serve with the eggs.

This & That

Any extras keep well in the refrigerator for a few days; simply reheat and serve as needed for a simple breakfast.

FRIED BANANA STUFFED FRENCH TOAST

Nut Free, Dairy Free

Growing up, French toast was always my favorite breakfast on weekends.
This version is made grain free using my sandwich bread and then stuffed with sweet fried bananas.
Serve with a side of crispy bacon for a complete breakfast treat!

SERVES 2-3

French Toast

6 slices Nut-Free Sandwich Bread
(page 30), sliced about ¾-inch (1.9-cm)
thick

4 eggs

¾ cup (178 ml) full-fat, unsweetened
coconut milk

1 tbsp (15 ml) raw honey

2 tsp (10 ml) vanilla extract

½ tsp ground cinnamon

Fried Bananas

2 slightly underripe bananas

¼ cup (58 g) butter, ghee or coconut oil

¼ tsp ground cinnamon

Maple syrup, for serving

Lightly toast the bread in the toaster oven for about a minute so that the bread is warm and soft. Because coconut flour is dense, this will help the batter soak into the bread.

Whisk together the eggs, coconut milk, honey, vanilla and cinnamon until smooth. Place the toast slices in a large, flat dish. Pour the batter over the toast and soak for 20 minutes, rotating once halfway through.

Meanwhile, heat a griddle or large skillet to medium heat and start making the fried bananas. Slice the bananas into ½-inch (1.3-cm) slices. Melt the butter on the griddle. Once the griddle is hot, arrange the banana slices, spreading evenly apart. Fry for 2 minutes, flip to the other side and fry for an additional 2 minutes or until the bananas are golden brown. Place the fried bananas on a plate and sprinkle with cinnamon.

Add the battered toast slices to the griddle, adding more butter if necessary. Cook for 2 minutes, flip to the other side and cook for an additional 2 minutes, or until both sides are golden brown.

Stuff the French toast with the fried bananas, plate and serve with a drizzle of maple syrup.

This & That
For a warm maple syrup recipe suggestion see page 44.

CRAB CAKE AND BACON SCRAMBLE HASH

Dairy Free, No Added Sugar

This hash is inspired by one of my favorite brunch spots in Southern California, Ramos House, a little farmhouse and patio tucked quietly away. As little girls, my sister and I used to ride the train up the coast with our mom on special occasions to have brunch. Their crab hash is famous and simply delightful, so I attempted to re-create it without the grains and dairy. Be sure to generously drizzle with Hollandaise!

SERVES 2 TO 4

Crab Cakes

¼ cup (25 g) almond flour

2 tbsp (28 g) Duck Fat Mayonnaise (page 152)

1 tbsp (9 g) fresh chives, minced

1 tsp (5 ml) lemon juice

1 tsp (6 g) Dijon mustard

½ tsp salt

½ tsp garlic powder

¼ tsp paprika

Few dashes of cayenne pepper, depending on preference

8 oz (227 g) jumbo lump crabmeat

2 tbsp (29 g) butter, ghee or coconut oil for frying cakes

Bacon Scramble

6 slices bacon

6 eggs

¼ cup (60 ml) full-fat unsweetened coconut milk or grass-fed heavy cream

¼ tsp (2 g) salt

2 handfuls fresh spinach

¼-½ cup (60-120 ml) Smoky Hollandaise Sauce (page 56), for serving

Warm a skillet to medium heat.

In the bottom of a bowl, mix together the almond flour, mayonnaise, chives, lemon juice, mustard and all remaining spices until you have created a thick batter. Add the crabmeat and stir to combine, being careful to not overmix, or your cakes will become mushy. Sometimes it is helpful to place the mixture in the refrigerator for 10 minutes before forming the cakes.

Melt the butter in the skillet, swirling around to coat the bottom. Use your hands to form the crab cakes into 4 round shapes. Carefully place them in the pan, allowing the butter to sizzle as they fry. Fry for 3 minutes and carefully flip to the other side for another 3 minutes or until your cakes are golden brown and cooked. Remove the cakes and place them on a wire rack (this helps prevent them from getting soggy).

Clean out the skillet, and cook the bacon for several minutes until both sides are crispy or to your desired preference. Whisk together the eggs, milk and salt. Crumble the bacon in the pan and add the egg batter and spinach. Turn the heat down to low and slowly scramble the eggs until cooked to your desired preference. Slowly stirring and folding the eggs will create a light and fluffy texture.

Plate the warm crab cakes with the bacon scramble on top. Garnish with a spoonful of hollandaise sauce.

SMOKY HOLLANDAISE SAUCE

Nut Free, No Added Sugar

Hollandaise sauce is full of nourishment and healthy fats, which are especially good for your brain and energy levels in the morning, and will keep you satisfied all day long. I love to serve a spoonful of this sauce over roasted vegetables for a bit of gourmet flavor. I use duck egg yolks because they have the creamiest taste, but you can also make this easily with regular egg yolks (see note), which I do when I don't have duck eggs on hand. Either way, this hollandaise is delicious and will have you wanting to eat it by the spoonful!

MAKES ABOUT ¾ CUP (180 ML) SAUCE

8 tbsp (115 g) butter or ghee

2 duck egg yolks*

2 tsp (10 ml) fresh lemon juice

⅛ tsp sea salt

⅛ tsp smoked paprika

Dash of cayenne pepper

You can substitute 3 regular egg yolks.

Add a cup (236 ml) of hot water to a blender, place the lid on top and set aside for 5 minutes.

Melt the butter in a small saucepan.

Pour out all the water from the blender and add the egg yolks, lemon juice, salt, paprika and cayenne pepper. Blend on high briefly, scrape down the sides and bottom of the blender and blend again briefly.

With the blender motor running on low speed, very slowly drizzle in the melted butter. This should take a few minutes, so be patient.

Store any remaining sauce in the refrigerator and simply heat and use as needed.

This & That

I usually keep a batch of this sauce on hand, because it can simplify breakfast preparation, especially when making the Steak and Egg Breakfast Fries (page 42) or crab hash (page 54), which require a few extra steps.

I love serving this sauce over roasted asparagus and topped with a poached egg for a nutritious meal at any time of the day.

Daily Gatherings

Everyday Comfort Food for Around the Table

These recipes are full of gourmet flavor that will take your everyday meals to a whole new level—comfort food with a healthy, tasty twist, as I like to say. Eating grain free does not mean eliminating all flavor or texture from your food. Quite the opposite, I think! There are many flavors and ingredients to choose from, but remember good-quality, fresh food will always taste the best. Take a moment to make a meal, gather and make memories around the table.

"This is the power of gathering: it inspires us, delightfully, to be more hopeful, more joyful, more thoughtful: in a word, more alive." —Alice Waters

SPAGHETTI AND MEATBALLS

Dairy Free, No Added Sugar

The ultimate comfort food, these meatballs are a great place to start if you are new to a grain-free and Paleo way of eating. They are simple, full of flavor and something everyone enjoys! Ground beef is an economical choice of meat, and I always keep grass-fed ground beef in my freezer for a simple weeknight dinner. Serve over spaghetti squash, spiraled zucchini (as pictured), roasted vegetables or even gluten-free noodles if you are hosting company and want to have options to make everyone comfortable!

MAKES 16 MEDIUM-SIZE MEATBALLS

Sauce

2 tbsp (30 ml) olive oil

½ small sweet yellow onion, chopped

2 large cloves garlic, crushed

1 tsp (3 g) fresh rosemary, chopped

1 tsp (3 g) dried oregano

½ tsp salt

28 oz (794 g) crushed tomatoes

15 oz (425 ml) tomato sauce

¼ cup (60 ml) good red wine (merlot or cabernet is best)

8 fresh basil leaves, chopped

Meatballs

2 tbsp (30 ml) olive oil or bacon grease, for frying

1 egg

1 tbsp (15 ml) balsamic vinegar

1½ tsp (8 g) salt

1 tsp (3 g) dried oregano

½ tsp fresh cracked black pepper

1 lb (454 g) ground beef

1 lb (454 g) pork Italian sausage, casings removed

¾ cup (73 g) almond flour

½ cup (68 g) finely shredded parmesan (optional), omit for dairy free

To make the sauce, warm a large stockpot to medium heat and add the olive oil. Sauté the onion, garlic, rosemary, oregano and salt for about 5 minutes or until the onions are translucent. Stir in the crushed tomatoes, tomato sauce, wine and basil. Reduce the heat to low, cover and simmer for 25 minutes.

Meanwhile, start making the meatballs. Warm a large skillet to medium heat and add the olive oil.

Place the egg, balsamic vinegar, salt, oregano and pepper in the bottom of a large mixing bowl. Whisk together. Add the ground beef, sausage, almond flour and parmesan to the bowl. Use your hands to crumble and mix together the meat until incorporated.

Next, shape the meatballs into medium-size round balls. Brown the meatballs in the skillet for 8 minutes, rotating so that all sides are browned. You may need to work in batches depending on the size of your skillet.

Once your tomato sauce has simmered, use an immersion blender to carefully puree the sauce. Drop the meatballs into the sauce, place the lid back on the pot and slowly simmer for 20 minutes.

Serve over your grain-free noodle of choice.

This & That

I prefer to use spicy Italian sausage because I think it adds incredible flavor to this dish. However, if you are serving this for children or prefer something with less kick to it, use mild or sweet Italian sausage.

CHIPOTLE TRI-TIP BOWLS

Nut Free, Dairy Free, No Added Sugar

Being that I'm from Southern California, Mexican food is always my favorite and my go-to meal. I love
making a hearty grain-free "burrito" bowl, usually with cauliflower rice as the base. This shredded tri-tip beef
has a bit of spice to it from the smoky chipotle peppers and is a great simple dinner, since it requires
little effort to prepare. Garnish with all your favorite taco fixings!

SERVES 4-6

3 dried chipotle peppers*

2 lb (907 g) tri-tip roast

½ tsp salt

¼ tsp fresh cracked black pepper

1 tbsp (12 g) bacon grease, for
browning meat

16 oz (454 g) fresh salsa

2 tbsp (17 g) tomato paste

1 lime, juiced

½ tsp dried oregano

Serving Suggestions
Mexican Spiced Rice (page 90)

Pico de Gallo (page 158)

Chopped lettuce

Guacamole (page 164) or avocado
slices

*For a less spicy version, use 2 chipotle
peppers.*

Preheat the oven to 225°F (107°C) and warm a Dutch oven to medium heat on the stove.

Slice the stems off the chipotle peppers, cut them open and remove the seeds. Soak
the peppers in a bowl of hot water for 15 minutes to soften.

Pat the roast dry with a paper towel and season both sides with salt and pepper. Melt
the bacon grease in the pan. Brown the roast for 2 minutes, flip to the other side and
continue searing for 2 additional minutes.

Add the salsa, tomato paste, lime juice, chipotle peppers and oregano to a blender.
Blend till smooth. Pour the salsa mixture on top, covering the roast.

Bake for 6 to 6½ hours or until the meat shreds apart easily with a fork. Shred the
meat in the pan, allowing it to soak up the sauce.

Serve over Mexican Spiced Rice with your desired toppings.

This & That

Tri-tip roasts are a delicious and cost-effective cut of meat, so this is one I
often try to buy grass-fed. I usually double this recipe and save extras for a
quick dinner or even scrambled into eggs for breakfast.

I typically buy a prepared locally made fresh salsa to save time. Just
double-check that the ingredients don't contain any added sugars or junk.

CHICKEN POT PIE AND BISCUITS

Dairy Free, No Added Sugar

When I first created the Morning Butter Biscuits (page 40), they were so delicious I couldn't stop eating them, so I wanted to create a recipe using them. This one is full of vegetables and fresh herbs, and it's the perfect comfort food. You can even substitute Smoked Turkey (page 204) if you have leftovers!

SERVES 6

3 skin-on chicken breasts (about 1¼ lbs [567 g])

1¼ tsp (7 g) salt, plus more for roasting chicken

1 tbsp (15 ml) olive oil

8 cremini mushrooms, minced

1 small sweet yellow onion, minced

1 cup (136 g) carrots, chopped

3 large cloves garlic, crushed

1 tsp (3 g) fresh rosemary, chopped

1 tsp (3 g) fresh thyme, chopped

1 tsp (3 g) fresh sage, chopped

½ tsp black pepper

1 cup (136 g) frozen green peas

1 cup (237 ml) coconut milk, full-fat and unsweetened

1 tsp (3 g) arrowroot flour

1 recipe Morning Butter Biscuit dough (page 40)

1 tbsp (15 g) melted butter, ghee or olive oil for brushing

Preheat the oven to 350°F (176°C). Sprinkle the skin side of the chicken breasts lightly with salt, cover the dish with foil and bake in the oven for 30 minutes.

Meanwhile, warm a large skillet on low heat and drizzle in the olive oil. Add the minced mushrooms, onions, carrots, garlic, rosemary, thyme, sage, salt and pepper. Sauté the vegetables for 15 to 20 minutes or until the carrots are tender and soft. Add the sauté mixture along with the peas to a large bowl and set aside. While everything is cooking, I usually prepare the biscuit dough.

When the chicken is finished cooking, allow it to cool for about 10 minutes before removing the skin and shredding the chicken. Add the chicken to the bowl with the vegetables and stir in the coconut milk and arrowroot until well mixed. Scoop the mixture into an 8 by 8 inch (20.3 by 20.3 cm) pan or medium oval baking dish.

Lightly oil your hands with coconut oil and shape the biscuit dough into small flat circles and arrange on top of the potpie filling. You may have extra dough, and if so, just use it to make a biscuit, according to baking instructions on page 40.

Lightly tent the dish with a piece of foil, place the chicken pot pie in the lower half of the oven and bake for 30 minutes, brushing the biscuit tops with the melted butter during the last 5 minutes of baking.

Cool for 10 minutes before serving.

This & That
To save time, you can prepare your chicken and chop your vegetables ahead of time.

CARNITAS

Nut Free, Dairy Free, No Added Sugar

A Southern California staple, carnitas, also known as "little meats," are great for weekday meals, because they basically cook themselves until the end, when you get to crisp them, creating the best texture! Not overly spiced, these carnitas are great to keep on hand, especially if feeding a large crowd. I like to use leftovers to turn into taco salads, mix into egg scrambles or add to Loaded Nachos (page 158).

SERVES 6-8

½ cup (118 ml) unsweetened apple juice

1 lime, juiced

3 cloves garlic, crushed

1 tbsp (15 g) salt

½ tsp black pepper

½ tsp ancho chili powder

½ tsp chipotle chili powder

½ tsp ground cumin

¼ tsp cayenne pepper

3 to 3½ lb (1361-1588 g) boneless pork shoulder roast

1 tbsp (15 ml) bacon grease, for searing

Soft Plantain Tortillas (page 84) or butter lettuce leaves for serving

Serving Suggestions

Pico de Gallo (page 158)

Guacamole (page 164)

Shredded lettuce

Roasted peppers

Full-fat sour cream

Cilantro

Lime wedges

Warm the oven to 250°F (121°C) and a Dutch oven to medium heat.

Whisk together the juices and garlic. In a separate bowl, mix together the salt and all other spices.

Slice the roast into 4 chunks. Sprinkle all sides with the salt seasoning.

Melt the bacon grease in the Dutch oven. Sear the pork for 1 minute, flip to the other side and sear for an additional minute (depending on the size of your pan, you may need to work in batches). Cover the meat with the juice mixture and place a lid on top.

Place in the oven and cook for 5 to 5½ hours or until the meat shreds apart easily, rotating the meat once halfway through.

Position the oven rack about 6 inches (15 cm) from the top of the oven. Turn up the oven temperature to broil.

Shred the pork with two forks and place the shredded meat, setting most of the juice to the side, on a rimmed baking sheet, spreading evenly apart so that the meat isn't piled up. Drizzle about ¼ cup (60 ml) of the juice on top. Broil for 6 minutes or until the carnitas are crispy to your liking.

Serve with tortillas topped your favorite taco garnishes—salsa, guacamole, cilantro, shredded lettuce or sour cream.

This & That

Carnitas are best in their fresh, crispy texture. If you are not planning on eating all the meat at once, broil the amount of meat you are going to eat and save the rest for later.

MEAT LOVERS SPAGHETTI SQUASH LASAGNA

Nut Free, Dairy Free, No Added Sugar

I honestly think I could eat this scrumptious one-pot wonder every day! Although there are no actual noodles in this lasagna, the flavors and texture are so delicious, you won't even notice the lack of real pasta. If you cannot tolerate dairy, simply omit the cheese. It tastes just as good.

SERVES 4

1 (3-lb [1361-g]) spaghetti squash

1 lb (454 g) spicy Italian sausage, casings removed

1 cup (136 g) marinara sauce*, preferably sugar free

1 cup (136 g) whole milk ricotta cheese

8 oz (227 g) whole milk mozzarella cheese, shredded

3 oz (85 g) pepperoni**

3 eggs, whisked

Italian herbs and fresh basil to garnish

I often have leftover sauce from Spaghetti and Meatballs (page 60), which I love using in this dish.

**I recommend Applegate brand.*

Preheat the oven to 375°F (190°C). Place the spaghetti squash in a baking dish and use the tip of a sharp knife to make several slices into the skin of the squash, allowing for heat to escape during baking. Bake for 35 to 40 minutes.

Allow the squash to cool for 10 minutes before slicing it open, removing and discarding the inside seeds. Use a fork to shred the squash into noodle-like strings. Now, transfer your spaghetti squash noodles to a nut milk bag or a fine mesh cloth and squeeze all the water out. You will eliminate a lot of liquid that otherwise will give your lasagna a soggy feel.

While the spaghetti squash is cooking, warm a large skillet to medium heat. Brown the sausage in the pan, crumbling into small pieces for about 5 minutes or until cooked. You want the sausage to be mostly cooked, but no need to worry about fully cooking it.

In a mixing bowl, mix together the shredded spaghetti squash and marinara sauce.

Now, you can start layering your lasagna in an 8 by 8 inch (20.3 by 20.3 cm) baking dish. Add half the spaghetti squash to the bottom of the dish, then add half the ricotta, sausage crumbles, mozzarella and pepperoni, in that order. Next add the remaining spaghetti squash, ricotta, and sausage crumbles. Pour the whisked egg evenly on top. Finally, add the remaining mozzarella and pepperoni.

Bake for 30 to 35 minutes or until the top is golden brown and a slight crust has formed around the edges. Garnish with Italian herbs and basil, if desired. Cool for 15 minutes before slicing and serving.

This & That

If you cannot tolerate dairy, you can still enjoy this dish: simply omit the cheeses. Because your dish will be smaller in scale, watch carefully so that the top does not burn!

Pre-shredded mozzarella is one of those cheeses that can sometimes contain added preservatives and even sawdust because it's highly processed. I recommend just buying a block of cheese and shredding it at home.

If you are very sensitive to spice, use sweet Italian sausage instead of spicy.

STEPHEN'S FIRE-GRILLED FILET MIGNON

Nut Free, Dairy Free, No Added Sugar

I definitely have to give my husband credit for this recipe, which is appropriately named after him!
This was the first meal he made for me when we were dating, and it is our favorite to cook when celebrating
or having friends over. Before Stephen, I was afraid to eat meat with any pink in it, but he slowly convinced
me to change my meat preference from well done to medium rare, which is the best way to eat a fillet
mignon, so resist the urge to cook it any longer. With any meat, the quality matters; but with steak,
the quality is especially important. So splurge a little, and rather than going out to a restaurant,
enjoy the perfect steak dinner in the comfort of your home.

SERVES 4

Steak Seasoning

3 tbsp (45 g) sea salt

3 tbsp (26 g) black pepper

1 tbsp (9 g) paprika

1 tsp (3 g) garlic powder

½ tsp onion powder

½ tsp dry mustard

⅛ tsp cayenne pepper

4 (8-oz [227-g]) filet mignon steaks

1 tbsp (15 ml) olive oil

2 tbsp (29 g) butter, for serving

Mix together all steak seasoning ingredients. Place the seasoning in a jar with a shaker lid.

Remove the steaks from the refrigerator and pat them dry with paper towels. Lightly coat all sides with olive oil. Sprinkle both sides of the steak with the steak seasoning. The amount of seasoning you use will depend on each person's preference; keep in mind that this seasoning has a bit of kick to it. Cover the steaks and set aside to come to room temperature for 1 hour.

After an hour, warm your barbecue to 550°F (287°C). Have a timer and grill tongs ready.

Place the steak on the grill at a 45-degree angle across the grates. Sear for 90 seconds, then flip to the other side and sear for an additional 90 seconds. Next, rotate the steak 45 degrees, flipping it back to the original side, and continue grilling for 90 seconds. Flip the steak one last time and grill for 90 seconds for a total of 6 minutes cooking time. Keep in mind the steaks will actually be on the grill for 7-8 minutes depending on how quickly you flip them. This process will create the perfect crisscross grill marks. Each time you open the grill to flip, be sure to work quickly and then close the grill door to prevent heat from escaping.

Remove the steaks from the grill, allowing them to rest for 10 minutes before serving. Top with a pat of butter as you plate, if desired.

Serve with Prosciutto-Wrapped Asparagus (page 80) and Smoky Roasted Sweet Potatoes (page 82) for the perfect steak dinner.

This & That

If you want the best taste, I recommend using natural fire from real firewood.

The recipe for steak seasoning is more than you will need, but you can keep extra in an airtight container to use when needed. I love to use this seasoning when roasting vegetables or sweet potatoes.

PAN-SEARED CAJUN SALMON

Nut Free, Dairy Free, No Added Sugar

A one-pan dinner on the table in 15 minutes—this dish is for you! Smoky Cajun seasoning gives this buttery salmon a most delicious flavor. I usually sauté fresh spinach in the pan after the fish is done for a simple, healthy meal.

SERVES 3-4

1 tbsp (15 g) butter or ghee*

1 lb (454 g) fresh, wild-caught salmon, cut into 4 fillets

1½ tsp (5 g) Cajun Seasoning (page 140)

3 fresh basil leaves, thinly sliced

*Use olive oil for strict dairy free

Warm a cast-iron skillet to medium heat for 5 minutes. Melt the butter in the pan, swirling around to coat the bottom and sides.

Season both sides of the salmon fillets with the cajun seasoning, rubbing most of the seasoning onto the skinless side.

Place the salmon in the hot pan, skin side down. Turn down the heat to medium-low. Sear for 6 minutes, without touching, or until the edges start to look cooked and slightly crispy. Carefully flip to the other side. This should be very easy and the skin should not stick to the bottom of the pan. Continue cooking for 3 to 4 minutes, depending on the size of your fillets. Keep in mind that the salmon will continue cooking as it is plated and served.

Serve over a bed of sautéed spinach or Rice Pilaf (page 90) and a garnish of basil.

FRIED CHICKEN COBB SALAD

Nut Free, Dairy Free, No Added Sugar

Cobb salad is forever my favorite, and I truly think I could eat this hearty, colorful salad every day!
This version takes things to a new level with the addition of fried chicken and crackling croutons.
Although the list of ingredients may seem long and involve a lot of preparation, I usually prepare
the ingredients separately and ahead of time so that you can just toss and serve!

SERVES 4-6

2 cups (272 g) fried chicken (page 128), cubed

1 cup (136 g) crackling pork belly croutons (page 86)

1 head romaine lettuce, shredded

1 large avocado, cubed

1 pint cherry tomatoes, sliced

4 green onions, chopped

4 oz (114 g) blue cheese, crumbled (omit for dairy free)

4 eggs, hard-boiled

¾ cup (178 ml) balsamic basil vinaigrette

Balsamic Basil Vinaigrette

1 cup (237 ml) olive oil

½ cup (118 ml) + 2 tbsp (30 ml) balsamic vinegar

⅓ cup (45 g) fresh basil leaves

2 tbsp (32 g) Dijon mustard

4 large cloves garlic

½ tsp salt

½ tsp black pepper

Start by preparing all your ingredients. Follow the instructions on page 168 to hard-boil the eggs. You can prepare the various ingredients ahead of time and simply refrigerate them in containers until you are ready to toss and serve.

To assemble, start by adding the lettuce to the bottom of a very large bowl. Next add the remaining ingredients, drizzling the appropriate amount of dressing on top. Store any remaining dressing in the refrigerator.

Lightly toss and serve.

This & That

Depending on what you have available and your desired taste, you could also use leftover filet mignon (page 70) or Smoked Turkey (page 204) in the salad.

HAWAIIAN-INSPIRED SESAME BRAISED SHORT RIBS

Nut Free, Dairy Free

Asian-flavored short ribs are a menu staple at restaurants here in Hawaii. However, most often the sauce is made with lots of sugar. That's not the case with this recipe. As the meat slow-cooks for hours, the short ribs simply fall apart with the touch of a fork. Short ribs are a simple meal to prepare and are absolute comfort food to me, but they're quite gourmet at the same time. Serve over Rice Pilaf (page 90) for a flavorful meal.

SERVES 3

2 lbs (907 g) boneless beef short ribs*

1¼ tsp (7 g) salt

¼ tsp black pepper

1 cup (237 ml) beef broth

4 tablespoons (60 ml) sesame oil

¼ cup (60 ml) coconut aminos

3 cloves garlic, crushed

1 tbsp (15 ml) raw honey

1 tbsp (15 ml) apple cider vinegar

1 tbsp (15 g) fresh ginger, minced

¼ tsp red chili pepper flakes

10 pearl onions, peeled

10 shiitake mushrooms, thinly sliced

Rice Pilaf (page 90), for serving

1 tsp (4 g) sesame seeds, for garnish

*I prefer boneless short ribs, because you get more meat. However, you can substitute 2½ to 3 pounds of bone-in short ribs.

Preheat the oven to 225°F (107°C). Warm a Dutch oven or pan to medium heat.

Season the ribs with salt and pepper. In a bowl, mix together the broth, 3 tablespoons (45 ml) of the sesame oil, coconut aminos, garlic, honey, apple cider vinegar, ginger and red chili pepper flakes.

Drizzle 1 tablespoon (15 ml) of sesame oil into the pan. Sear the ribs for 1 minute per side, flip and continue searing for an additional minute on the other side. Depending on the size of your pan, you may need to work in batches.

Remove the pan from heat and cover the ribs in the sauce, onions and mushrooms, stirring to mix together. Cover with a lid and place in the oven.

Bake for 5½ to 6½ hours or until the meat shreds apart easily with a fork, rotating the ribs halfway through. If the meat is not very tender to touch, continue cooking for 30 minutes.

Serve hot over Rice Pilaf and garnish with sesame seeds.

GRILLED CHICKEN KABOBS
WITH PROSCIUTTO-WRAPPED PEACHES

Nut Free, Dairy Free, No Added Sugar

Sweet and savory combinations are my absolute favorite, and these juicy kabobs achieve just that! In the fall,
I usually replace the peaches with pears or whatever fruit is in season. This meal is quite simple to prepare,
and I usually double the recipe to save for lunches or if serving to dinner guests. Serve over
a bed of Rice Pilaf (page 90) for a completely satisfying meal.

SERVES 3

1 lb (454 g) chicken breasts

1 tbsp (15 ml) olive oil

1 tsp (3 g) fresh rosemary, chopped

½ tsp salt

½ tsp garlic powder

1 peach, slightly underripe

3 oz (85 g) prosciutto, thinly sliced

2 tbsp (30 ml) balsamic glaze/reduction

Slice the chicken into small cubes about 1-inch (2.5-cm) thick. Toss together with the olive oil, rosemary, salt and garlic. Marinate in the refrigerator for 30 minutes to 1 hour.

When you are ready to grill, warm your grill to medium heat (between 400 and 450°F [204 and 233°C]).

Cut the peach into slices and the prosciutto in half lengthwise. Wrap each peach slice with a piece of prosciutto.

Thread the chicken and prosciutto-wrapped peaches onto kabob skewers, alternating with a few chunks of chicken, then a peach.

Grill for 3 to 3½ minutes, flip to the other side and grill for an additional 3 to 3½ minutes, depending on the thickness of your chicken and heat of the grill.

Drizzle with balsamic glaze and serve.

This & That
Balsamic glaze or reduction is a thick, sweet syrup and easy to find in most stores. Just watch out—sometimes the ingredients can be questionable.

PROSCIUTTO-WRAPPED ASPARAGUS

Nut Free, Dairy Free, No Added Sugar

In our house, we refer to these as the "healthy French fries!" No matter if it is a simple weeknight dinner or a dinner party for guests, these asparagus are simply delightful and a great way to add some healthy comfort food to your table. A thinner asparagus will yield the best texture and flavor; thick asparagus can sometimes be a bit tough.

SERVES 6

1 bunch thin asparagus

6 oz (170 g) thinly sliced prosciutto slices

1 tbsp (15 ml) olive oil

Salt and black pepper to taste

Preheat the oven to 400°F (204°C).

Cut the tough bottom ends off the asparagus spears. Take 3 asparagus and tightly wrap them in a prosciutto slice. Place on a baking sheet and repeat with the remaining asparagus and prosciutto.

Lightly drizzle with olive oil and sprinkle with salt and pepper.

Roast for 10 minutes, flipping the asparagus bundles halfway through.

This & That

I highly recommend using thin asparagus for the best taste and texture, but if you can only find thicker ones you may need to individually wrap the asparagus and increase the cooking time by about 3 to 5 minutes.

SMOKY ROASTED SWEET POTATOES

Nut Free, Dairy Free, No Added Sugar

Whenever I serve these to friends, I am always asked how I make them taste so yummy. Truth is,
I don't really have a recipe, I just follow my personal favorite cooking advice: "When in doubt, more butter,
more salt and more garlic!" So the best part is that you don't really need a recipe, just make sure
to add lots of butter or your fat of choice.

SERVES 4

3 large sweet potatoes

2 tbsp (30 ml) olive oil

2 tsp (12 g) salt

½ tsp garlic powder

¼ tsp paprika

¼ tsp smoked paprika

4 tbsp (58 g) butter or ghee*

*Use bacon grease or duck fat for dairy
free.

Preheat the oven to 400°F (204°C).

Cut the sweet potatoes into small cubes, about ½-inch (1.3-cm) thick. Place on a baking sheet and toss together with the olive oil, salt and seasonings. Cut the butter into very small cubes and arrange on top of the potatoes.

Roast for 40 minutes, stirring halfway though.

Serve as a dinner side dish and save any extras for scrambling into eggs the next morning.

This & That

If I have Steak Seasoning (page 70) or Cajun Seasoning (page 140) on hand, I often season the potatoes with them to save time.

Whenever you cook bacon, always save your bacon grease. It adds great flavor to these roasted sweet potatoes or any roasted vegetables.

SOFT PLANTAIN TORTILLAS

Nut Free, Dairy Free, No Added Sugar

Sometimes you just need a tortilla shell to fill with your favorite meats and toppings. These tortillas are made with plantains and are soft, yet can be filled to the brim without tearing.

MAKES 10 TORTILLAS

---

2 yellow plantains (not overly ripe), peeled and cubed

1 egg + 1 egg white

1 tbsp (15 g) butter, ghee or coconut oil, melted

¼ tsp salt

Preheat the oven to 400°F (204°C). Line two baking sheets with parchment paper and set aside.

Add all ingredients to a blender or the bowl of a food processor.

Blend the tortilla batter for about 30 seconds, scrape down the sides of the bowl and briefly blend again until completely smooth.

Use a tablespoon measurer to scoop two heaping full scoops onto the prepared baking sheets, leaving about 5 inches (13 cm) between each tortilla. Next use the back of the tablespoon or a small spatula to smooth out the tortilla batter, moving in a circular motion until you have created a thin layer.

Bake for 8 minutes, then carefully remove the baking sheet from the oven, flip the tortillas and continue baking for an additional 4 minutes, watching carefully at the end so that the edges do not burn.

Fill with your favorite taco toppings!

This & That

The key to keeping these tortillas soft and pliable is to thinly spread out the batter with a spatula. Be patient. This can take some time, but the end result is worth it!

Like most grain-free baked goods, these are best served fresh and warm.

CRACKLING PORK BELLY CROUTONS

Nut Free, Dairy Free, No Added Sugar

Slightly crunchy and slightly salty, these crackling croutons will have you wanting to eat them by the handful. Although traditional croutons are made with bread, these croutons turn pork belly into crackling, savory bites of deliciousness. I wanted to keep this recipe simple so that you can enjoy croutons without all the extra baking steps. Add a heaping spoonful to classic Caesar Salad (page 88) or Tomato Basil Soup (page 190), or watch them quickly disappear straight from the pan!

MAKES ABOUT 4 CUPS (545 G)

2 lb (907 g) pork belly

2½ tsp (13 g) sea salt

1 tsp (3 g) fresh cracked black pepper

1 tsp (3 g) garlic powder

Herbed Crouton Option

½ tsp fresh rosemary, chopped

½ tsp fresh thyme, chopped

Cut the pork belly into ½-inch (1.3-cm) cubes. Sprinkle the salt, pepper and garlic over the cubes, tossing together so that all sides are evenly seasoned. Place in a sealable bag and then in the refrigerator to marinate for 8 hours or overnight.

When you are ready to cook, remove the pork belly from the refrigerator and bring to room temperature for 20 minutes. Warm a large cast-iron or nonstick skillet to medium heat.

Place the pork belly in the skillet, evenly arranging so that all of it touches the heat. You may have to work in batches, depending on the size of your skillet.

Sear for 3 minutes without touching, then flip to the other side and continue searing for an additional 3 minutes. Give the pork belly a stir and continue cooking for 2 additional minutes, stirring constantly to ensure that all sides are golden brown.

Remove the croutons with a slotted spoon and place them on a paper towel. If you are making the herbed croutons, toss in the herbs while the pork belly is still warm.

Use as needed and store remaining croutons in the refrigerator.

This & That

Croutons are best served immediately, because that is when they are the most crunchy. If you are storing extras in the refrigerator, lightly heat them up in a skillet or the oven as needed.

CAESAR SALAD

Nut Free, Dairy Free, No Added Sugar

Here, I combine crisp romaine and crunchy croutons for a simple salad full of flavor and texture.
I usually keep a bottle of this dressing on hand to use throughout the week
because it makes eating salad so delicious.

SERVES 6

Dressing

1 cup (236 ml) olive oil

2 egg yolks

2 tbsp (30 ml) balsamic vinegar

1½ tbsp (24 ml) Dijon mustard

1 tbsp (15 ml) lemon juice

4 large cloves garlic, crushed

½ tsp sea salt

½ tsp black pepper

Few dashes of cayenne pepper, to taste

1 head romaine lettuce, shredded

1 cup (136 g) Crackling Pork Belly
Croutons (page 86)

3 green onions, chopped

Parmesan cheese shavings, omit for
dairy free

Mix together all the dressing ingredients until thick, creamy and smooth.

In a large bowl, add your shredded romaine lettuce, croutons, green onions and Parmesan shavings, if desired. Toss together with desired amount of dressing.

Store your leftover dressing in the refrigerator for 5 days.

CAULIFLOWER RICE—THREE FLAVORS

Nut Free, Dairy Free, No Added Sugar

I used to have a fear of the white, tree-like vegetable cauliflower, but now this "rice" is a staple in our house and can be created with almost any seasonings. It makes the perfect side dish to many of the entrées found in this book.

SERVES 4-6

Basic Cauliflower Rice

4 tbsp (58 g) butter or ghee*

1 large head cauliflower

1 tsp (5 g) Celtic sea salt

Rice Pilaf

2 large carrots, finely chopped

4 green onions, finely chopped

1 cup (136 g) green peas

2 large cloves garlic, crushed

Mexican Spiced Rice

½ small white onion, minced

2 tbsp (9 g) fresh cilantro, finely chopped

1 tbsp (15 ml) fresh lime juice

*Use olive oil for strict dairy-free.

Warm a large skillet to medium heat, melting the butter in the pan. If you are making the Rice Pilaf, sauté the carrots for 20 minutes or until soft. If making the Mexican Spiced Rice, sauté the white onion for 20 minutes or until soft.

Cut the cauliflower into small florets, discarding the outer leaves and inner core. Using the grating attachment of a food processor, shred the cauliflower into "rice."

Add the cauliflower rice and salt to the warm pan, sautéing for 20 minutes or until soft. During the last 5 minutes, stir in any remaining ingredients of your chosen flavor.

Serve warm.

CHEWY HAZELNUT CHOCOLATE CHUNK COOKIES

Dairy Free

Oh, these little cookies—this was one of the recipes that inspired me to write this book when my husband was deployed a few years back. Over many emails back and forth during this time, he kept requesting healthy chocolate chip cookies, so I created these using a handful of different flours. Because they are a weekly request in our house, they are purposefully not overly sweet and are quite simple to make. You can even make them into ice cream sandwiches or crumble a few over Vanilla Ice Cream (page 144).

MAKES 12 COOKIES

4 tbsp (58 g) butter or palm shortening for dairy free

1 egg

3 tbsp (38 g) coconut sugar

1 tbsp (15 ml) raw honey

1 tsp (5 ml) vanilla extract

¾ cup (64 g) hazelnut flour

½ cup (55 g) almond flour

1½ tbsp (9 g) coconut flour

½ tsp baking soda

Pinch of salt

½ cup (70 g) dark chocolate chunks*

I recommend using Pure7 chocolate bars because they are minimally sweetened with raw honey.

Preheat the oven to 350°F (176°C). Line a baking sheet with parchment paper.

Slice the butter into 4 pieces and set aside to soften for 15 minutes. Set the egg on the counter to bring it to room temperature.

In a mixing bowl, use a hand mixer to cream the butter, coconut sugar, honey and vanilla extract until smooth and fluffy. Add the egg and mix briefly.

Next, add the flours, baking soda and salt. Blend, scrape down the sides and bottom of the bowl and briefly blend again. Add the chocolate chunks and use a spatula to fold them in by hand.

Use a 1½ tablespoon (23 g) cookie scoop to scoop cookie dough onto the baking sheet, placing the cookies a few inches apart from each other. Very lightly, press down on the tops of the cookies, flattening them ever so slightly. They will not rise or expand much, but this helps them cook evenly.

Bake for 11 to 13 minutes, watching carefully at the end. Cool cookies on the baking sheet for 5 minutes, resisting the urge to touch or eat them, because this helps the cookies firm up. Transfer to a cooling rack.

Eat and enjoy warm and fresh from the oven!

This & That

These cookies are best eaten warm and out of the oven, but if you need to store them, be sure to place them in a cool location.

LEMON CURD CELEBRATION CAKE

Nut Free

This was the cake that started my blog Colorful Eats as well as my passion for creating healthy recipes. I designed this cake for our wedding because although I cannot eat grains or refined sugars, I still wanted to be able to be a normal bride and cut a cake with my husband. Pretty soon after, everyone started asking for the recipe, and every time I make this cake, it brings me so much joy to watch my friends and family devour slice after slice, usually without even knowing it's grain-free! So whatever you are celebrating—birthdays, weddings, babies or just the fact that life deserves to be celebrated every day—have a slice of cake!

MAKES 1 DOUBLE-LAYER 9 INCH (22.8 CM) CAKE

Lemon Curd

8 tbsp (115 g) butter

5 egg yolks

½ cup (119 ml) fresh squeezed lemon juice

¼ cup (85 ml) raw honey

Pinch of sea salt

Cake Ingredients

Coconut oil, for greasing pan

1 cup (100 g) coconut flour, sifted

1 tsp (5 g) baking soda

¼ tsp sea salt

8 eggs

6 tbsp (86 g) butter, melted

¾ cup (184 g) plain, whole milk yogurt or coconut yogurt

¼ cup (59 ml) raw honey

2 tbsp (30 ml) fresh squeezed lemon juice

1 tbsp (10 g) fresh lemon zest

2 tsp (10 ml) vanilla extract

8 oz (228 ml) grass-fed heavy whipping cream or whipped coconut cream*

1 pound (450 g) fresh berries of choice

*See explanation on page 132.

In a medium saucepan or double boiler over low heat, melt the butter. In a separate bowl, whisk together the egg yolks, lemon juice, raw honey and salt until smooth. Once the butter has melted, pour in the egg yolk mixture. Continue heating, stirring constantly, for about 15 minutes or until the curd begins to steam and thicken. Be careful—you do not want the curd to burn or to allow it to simmer.

Transfer the lemon curd to a clean bowl and allow it to cool for 20 minutes before covering it and placing in the refrigerator for a minimum of 4 hours.

When you are ready to bake the cake, preheat your oven to 350°F (176°C) and brush the sides and bottom of a 9 inch (22.8 cm) round cake pan with coconut oil.

In a mixing bowl, sift together the coconut flour, baking soda and sea salt. In a separate bowl, use a hand mixer to blend together the eggs, melted butter, yogurt, honey, lemon juice, zest and vanilla until smooth.

Add the flour to the egg batter and blend until smooth. Scrape down the sides and bottom of the bowl and blend again on high for about 20 seconds. This will trap air, helping the cake to rise evenly.

Pour the batter into the prepared cake pan. Bake for 40 to 45 minutes or until a tester comes out clean, keeping in mind that the cake will continue to cook even after it is out of the oven. Remove the pan from the oven, placing it on a cooling rack for 30 minutes before carefully inverting it onto the cooling rack to cool completely.

Once the cake is cool and the lemon curd has set, use a long, sharp knife to carefully slice the cake in half. Make the whipped cream by using beaters or a hand mixer to whip the cream until soft, foamy peaks begin to form.

Now it's time to torte the cake. Place half of the cake onto a serving dish, spreading a layer of lemon curd on top. Add half the whipped cream and spread out evenly. Next, add a few handfuls of fresh berries. Place the other half of the cake on top and repeat this process of layering and garnishing with berries.

If you are not going to eat the cake right away, be sure to keep it in the refrigerator.

Slice and serve!

A Red, White & Blue Table

Celebrating American Heroes

Nothing says American quite like a big barbecue bash! Do not limit these recipes to Fourth of July or summertime only; many are staples in our house. Invite some friends over, light the smoker, pour a margarita and enjoy—remembering those who serve and sacrificed!

"Honor the soldier and sailor everywhere, who bravely bears his country's cause."
—President Lincoln

SMOKED BABY BACK RIBS

Nut Free, Dairy Free

My husband and I had so much fun creating this recipe together. I can honestly say it is our absolute favorite recipe in this book! These smoked ribs are dry-rubbed so that you can really enjoy the smoky flavor of the meat. Invite over some friends, be sure to grab some paper towels and dig in—these are finger-lickin' good!

SERVES 8

2 (3 lb [1361 g]) racks pork baby back ribs

1 tbsp (15 ml) mustard

½ cup (68 g) Smoker Dry Rub Seasoning (page 120)

½ cup (118 ml) unsweetend apple juice, in a spray bottle

Kicking Barbecue Sauce (page 118), for serving

This & That

Every cooking environment and rack of ribs are different. The cooking time will vary, so be sure to trust the internal temperature reading, taking temperature readings in various locations because the bones can create inaccuracies.

Although I prefer the taste of hickory-smoked ribs, you can also smoke with a fruit wood like apple or cherry.

One day prior to smoking, start preparing the ribs. First, remove the membrane from the underside of the ribs by sliding a thin knife under the membrane and between the bones. Lift and loosen the membrane until is starts to tear, then peel back the entire layer. Pat the ribs dry with paper towels.

Next, place the mustard in your hands and rub on a thin layer, covering all sides of the ribs. Generously season all sides of the ribs with the smoker dry rub. Wrap the ribs in foil and refrigerate for 24 hours.

When you are ready to smoke, remove the ribs from the refrigerator, for 30–45 minutes, allowing them to come to room temperature. Prepare the smoker with hickory wood and light the fire, bringing the smoker's internal temperature to a stable 225°F (107°C).

Place the ribs on the grill grates, meat side up. Smoke for 2 hours. Make sure to constantly tend to the fire to maintain the heat of 225°F (107°C). If the temperature drops too low, it will be difficult to maintain.

Next, prepare a few sheets of foil. Generously spritz the ribs with the apple juice, then tightly wrap the ribs in foil. You will want to do this quickly so that your meat does not loose too much heat. Continue smoking for 2 hours.

Unwrap the ribs and place back on the smoker grates, spritizing with juice one last time. When you unwrap, the internal temperature will be about 175 to 180°F (79 to 82°C) and the meat will be starting to separate from the bone.

Smoke for an additional 30 minutes to 1 hour, maintaining over 185°F (82°C) internal temperature. Once the ribs reach 195°F (90°C), pull them off.

Allow the ribs to rest for 15 minutes before cutting and serving with Kicking Barbecue Sauce.

HONEY LIME MARGARITAS

Nut Free, Dairy Free, No Added Sugar

I will be honest, margaritas are my absolute favorite. I don't drink often, or recommend anyone drinking often, but sometimes I feel like life calls for the occasion and truly deserves to be celebrated! On the weekends, my husband and I love to grill together, and this drink is perfect to sip on a hot day. I prefer mine without any added sugar, so he came up with an entirely fruit-sweetened margarita for me. If you love having people over, this margarita is great for entertaining. Drinks have a way of bringing people together, and we love making this for friends while waiting for dinner to finish. I highly recommend using good quality tequila and fresh-squeezed juices. They are what make these margaritas so great. Cheers!

MAKES 1 MARGARITA

Classic Margarita

2 oz (60 ml) fresh-squeezed lime juice

1½ oz (45 ml) pure agave gold tequila

¾ oz (23 ml) Honey Simple Syrup (page 122)

Fruit Sweetened Margarita

2 oz (60 ml) fresh-squeezed lime juice

1 oz (30 ml) fresh-squeezed orange juice

1½ oz (45 ml) pure agave gold tequila

Cadillac Margarita

Float 1 oz (30 ml) Grand Marnier on top of the margarita

Ice to fill the shaker and cups

Lime slices, for the rims and garnish

Salt for the rims, if desired

Add all ingredients of either the classic margarita or fruit-sweetened margarita to a cocktail shaker. Add two handfuls of ice to the shaker and shake for 10 seconds.

Rub a lime slice around the rim of the glass, then dip the glass in the salt, if a salted rim is desired. Next, fill the glass with ice. Pour the contents of the shaker into the ice-filled glass. If you want to make the Cadillac margarita, float the Grand Marnier on top of the margarita.

Garnish with a slice of lime.

Best sipped immediately.

This & That

For the smoothest taste, I recommend using only reposado or añjeo tequila, which is an aged, gold tequila. Whatever you decide, I do not recommend using silver tequila.

Grand Marnier is a French type of orange liqueur and, in my opinion, offers the best taste; however you can also use Curaçao or Cointreau.

SLOW-COOKED PULLED PORK SANDWICHES

Nut Free, Dairy Free

This is one of my favorite dishes to serve to guests, because you can toss it together in the morning
and let it slow-cook all day, filling your house with the most lovely, smoky flavor!
Add a spoonful to toasted Sandwich Rolls (page 150) and top with Cole Slaw (page 110).

SERVES 6-8

2 tsp (10 g) salt

½ tsp black pepper

½ tsp paprika

¼ tsp smoked paprika

¼ tsp garlic powder

¼ tsp dried thyme

1 cup (136 g) Kicking Barbecue
Sauce (page 118)

1 tbsp (15 ml) liquid smoke,
hickory flavor

3½ lb (1588 g) boneless pork
shoulder roast

Sandwich Rolls (page 150), for serving

Cole Slaw (page 110), for serving

Preheat the oven to 225°F (107°C). Add all the salt and seasonings to a small bowl
and mix together to prepare the dry rub. Whisk together the barbecue sauce and
liquid smoke.

Season all sides of the roast with the dry rub, using your fingers to massage into the
meat. Add the meat to a Dutch oven or baking dish similar to the size of the roast.
Pour the barbecue sauce and liquid smoke over the roast, placing a lid on top of the
pan. If you do not have a lid to fit your pan, you can also place a sheet of foil over
the top, tightly securing it so that no heat escapes.

Bake for 8 hours or until the pork shreds apart easily with a fork. Shred the meat into
the sauce, allowing it to soak up the sauce for several minutes before serving.

Serve with the sandwich rolls and a scoop of cole slaw.

This & That

If you do not have time to make the rolls, you can serve this meat with
Smoky Roasted Sweet Potatoes (page 82).

For a nut-free serving option, serve over sliced Nut-Free Sandwich Bread
(page 30).

RED, WHITE & BLUE SALAD

Nut Free, Dairy Free, No Added Sugar

This recipe was inspired by the salad that was served at our wedding, which was actually called the "Red, White & Blue" salad. My husband absolutely loves it, and I promise it will have everyone reaching for a second helping of leafy greens!

SERVES 6

---

5 oz (142 g) fresh spring mix

8 oz (227 g) fresh strawberries, sliced

3 oz (85 g) fresh blueberries

6 oz (170 g) feta cheese, crumbled*

½ cup (34 g) toasted pecan pieces (omit for nut free)

¼ red onion, thinly sliced

2 tbsp (17 g) fresh basil, finely chopped

½ cup (118 ml) Balsamic Basil Vinaigrette (page 74)

*Traditional Greek feta is made from sheep or goat milk, which for some people can be easier to digest. If you cannot tolerate dairy of any kind, simply omit the cheese.

Add all salad ingredients, except the vinaigrette, to a very large bowl.

Just as you are about to serve, drizzle on the balsamic vinaigrette and lightly toss.

SKILLET PEACH COBBLER

Dairy Free

Because peach season only comes once a year, take advantage of all the fresh peaches while you can! This cobbler can be whisked up in minutes and is great to serve for parties. Make it à la mode by adding a scoop of Vanilla Ice Cream (page 144).

SERVES 6-8

8 tbsp (115 g) butter or ghee*

2 lbs (907 g) fresh peaches

2 tbsp (17 g) arrowroot flour

1½ cups (145 g) cashew flour

3 tbsp (38 g) coconut sugar

½ tsp baking powder

2 tbsp (30 ml) raw honey

Vanilla Ice Cream (page 144), for serving

For a dairy-free option, use palm shortening, although I prefer the taste with butter.

Preheat the oven to 350°F (176°C) and arrange the baking rack in the middle of the oven.

Slice the butter into small cubes and set aside to come to room temperature for 20 minutes.

Peel the peaches, removing the pits and slicing each peach into about 8 slices. Place the peaches in a bowl and toss together with the arrowroot flour.

Stir together the cashew flour, coconut sugar and baking powder. Add in the softened butter and honey using a fork or pasty cutter to form a loose ball of dough.

Add the peaches to a 10 inch (25.4 cm) skillet. Use a spoon to crumble the dough on top of the peaches. Lightly tent with a piece of foil.

Bake for 20 minutes, remove the foil and continue baking for an additional 23 to 25 minutes or until the entire crust starts to turn golden brown. Watch carefully—cashew flour can burn easily.

Cool for 10 minutes before serving with a scoop of ice cream!

SMOKER-STYLE BRISKET

Nut Free, Dairy Free

They say that good things come to those who wait, and this brisket recipe stays true to that statement.
It takes a lot of work to smoke, but the result is incredible, and what I like to refer to as "meat candy." As with
all meat, the quality really matters. Starting with a good quality of meat will result in a better end texture.
It is a fun project to have going during the day if you are hanging out at the house,
but be sure to invite friends over to share in the feast!

SERVES 6-10

1 (7-lb [3176 g]) beef brisket, with a good fat cap

1 tbsp (15 ml) olive oil

½ cup (68 g) Smoker Dry Rub Seasoning (page 120)

1 cup (235 ml) unsweetened apple juice mixed with 2 tbsp (30 ml) apple cider vinegar, for spraying and injecting

Kicking Barbecue Sauce (page 118), for serving

This & That

If you are measuring the internal temperature, there is a chance that the brisket will rise steadily until about 160°F (65°C), then it will stall and climb slowly. Be patient with the last few degrees, because it can take a while.

You can choose a brisket of any size. Just adjust the seasoning amount and cooking time accordingly, making sure to trust the internal temperature reading.

At about 185°F (85°C), the meat collagens start to break down, creating the most tender, melt-in-your-mouth texture, which is why the internal temperature is so important to achieve.

One day prior to smoking, start preparing the brisket. Pat the brisket dry with paper towels. Lightly coat the entire brisket with olive oil and generously rub all sides with the dry rub.

Wrap the brisket in foil and place in the refrigerator to marinate for 24 hours.

When you are ready to smoke, remove the brisket from the refrigerator and set aside for 1 hour to come to room temperature. During this time, prepare the smoker with mesquite wood, bringing the smoker's internal temperature to a stable 225°F (107°C).

Just before you begin smoking, inject the brisket with a bit of apple juice mixture in various spots.

Place the brisket on the smoker grates, fat side up.

Smoke the brisket for 3 hours, spritzing with apple juice and injecting once halfway through. Constantly tend to the fire, adding fuel when necessary to prevent the temperature from dropping too low.

Next, work quickly to tightly wrap the brisket in foil, spraying with apple juice once again and making sure there are no holes so that the moisture doesn't escape. Continue smoking for 2 hours, maintaining the 225°F (107°C) temperature. Unwrap the brisket and smoke for an additional hour or until the internal temperature reaches 195°F (90°C) After unwrapping, you may have already reached the desired internal temperature, so simply smoke for a lesser amount of time, because this end process creates the most fabulous outer texture.

Allow the brisket to rest for 20 minutes before slicing against the grain.

Serve with Kicking Barbecue Sauce.

COLE SLAW

Nut Free, Dairy Free

The epitome of a summer side dish and great for feeding a large, hungry crowd, this cole slaw
goes perfectly with any of the smoked meat dishes in this chapter.

SERVES 8-10

⅔ cup (90 g) Duck Fat Mayonnaise
(page 152)

1 tbsp (15 ml) apple cider vinegar

1 tbsp (15 ml) fresh squeezed lemon
juice

1 tbsp (15 ml) Dijon mustard

1 tbsp (15 ml) raw honey

1 tsp (5 g) salt

½ tsp black pepper

½ green cabbage, thinly sliced

½ red cabbage, thinly sliced

2 large carrots, shredded

2 green onions, chopped

Whisk together the mayonnaise, apple cider vinegar, lemon juice, mustard, honey,
salt and pepper.

Add all the vegetables to a very large bowl. Drizzle in the dressing and toss together.

Refrigerate the cole slaw for 30 minutes to allow the flavors to marinate together.

Toss one last time and serve.

GRILLED MAHI-MAHI FISH TACOS

Nut Free, Dairy Free, No Added Sugar

The simplicity of this dish allows the flavor of fresh fish to shine through. If you do not have tortillas on hand,
serve the fish in lettuce cups, which makes for a light and summery dish made entirely on the grill!

SERVES 3

1 tbsp (15 ml) olive oil

1 tbsp (15 ml) fresh-squeezed lime juice

1 tsp (5 g) salt

½ tsp ground cumin

½ tsp garlic powder

¼ tsp chili powder*

1 lb (454 g) fresh mahi-mahi fillet

For serving

Butter lettuce leaves or Soft Plantain
Tortillas (page 84)

Fresh mango, cubed

Pico de Gallo (page 158)

1 avocado, sliced

Cilantro

Shredded cabbage

*Omit for nightshade-free

Mix together the olive oil, lime juice, salt, cumin, garlic and chili powder. Place
the fish in a shallow dish, covering with the marinade. Coat both sides evenly and
marinate in the refrigerator for 30 minutes to 1 hour.

When you are ready to grill, warm your barbecue to medium-high heat (between
400 and 450°F [204 and 232°C]). Place the fish on the grill, basting with half of the
remaining marinade. Grill for 3 to 3½ minutes, flip to the other side, basting with the
remaining marinade. Grill for an additional 3 to 3½ minutes.

Remove the fish from the grill, flaking the fish apart and filling your tacos. Top with
any desired toppings.

This & That
Fresh fish truly makes all the difference—if you cannot find mahi-mahi, you
can also use swordfish, halibut or other types of flaky white fish.

MELON CAPRESE LOLLIPOPS

Nut Free, Dairy Free, No Added Sugar

My absolute favorite appetizer or snack in the summertime, this dish requires no cooking
and little preparation, so it is perfect for a hot day. I added salty prosciutto to this classic Caprese salad
for those who cannot have dairy, and it's a nice touch!

SERVES 8

½ large cantaloupe melon

6 oz (170 g) prosciutto slices

8 oz (227 g) ciliegine mozzarella*
(small mozzarella balls)

1 pint (322 g) cherry tomatoes*

2 tbsp (30 ml) olive oil

2 tbsp (30 ml) balsamic vinegar

Salt and pepper, to taste

½ cup (68 g) fresh basil, sliced

Toothpicks, for assembling

*For dairy- or nightshade-free, replace
the mozzarella and tomatoes with
cubed avocados

Remove the seeds from the cantaloupe. Use a 1 tablespoon (15 g) scooper to scoop
the melon into small balls.

Layer prosciutto slices, melon, mozzarella and tomato, sticking a toothpick through
the center to hold together.

Drizzle with olive oil and balsamic vinegar. Sprinkle with salt and pepper to taste.

Garnish with fresh basil.

This & That

The lollipops can be prepared ahead of time, simply add the dressing and
basil just as you are about to serve.

TOASTED COCONUT LEMON TARTS

Nut Free

Slightly tart and tangy, these lemon tarts are fabulously topped with fresh summer berries!
The bright yellow lemon adds a pop of color to your table.

MAKES SIX 4½-INCH (11.5-CM) TARTS OR ONE 9-INCH (23-CM) ROUND TART

2 cups (160 g) finely shredded, unsweetened coconut flakes

3 tbsp (45 ml) coconut oil

3 tbsp (45 ml) raw honey

1 tbsp (6 g) + 1 tsp (2 g) coconut flour

1 tsp (5 ml) vanilla extract

Zest of one lemon

Lemon Curd Filling

12 tbsp (172 g) butter

¾ cup (178 ml) fresh-squeezed lemon juice

¼ cup (60 ml) + 2 tbsp (30 ml) raw honey

4 egg yolks

1 tbsp (9 g) grass-fed gelatin

Fresh berries

Preheat the oven to 350°F (176°C).

Add all the crust ingredients to the bowl of a food processor and pulse several times until mixed and crumbly.

Spoon the coconut mixture into a tart pan with a removable bottom (if the pan is not nonstick, you will need to brush with coconut oil). Use a small spatula or the tips of your fingers to evenly and firmly press into the bottom and sides of the tart pan. Be patient with the process—it is what makes the crust stick together.

Bake for 9 to 12 minutes or until the crust is golden brown. Set aside to cool completely.

While the crust is baking, begin making the lemon curd filling. Over the low heat of a double boiler, melt the butter. In a separate bowl, whisk together the lemon juice, honey and egg yolks. Once the butter is completely melted, whisk in the lemon juice mixture.

Stirring continuously, heat the lemon curd for 10 minutes. Next, sprinkle the gelatin evenly on top of the warm curd and continue heating and stirring for an additional 10 minutes or until the gelatin is completely dissolved. Set aside to cool for 20 minutes.

Slowly pour the lemon curd filling into the coconut crust, then carefully transfer to the refrigerator to chill for 4 hours.

Top with fresh berries, slice and enjoy!

This & That

Because of the coconut oil, the crust will harden as it cools, so I recommend taking it out of the refrigerator 5 minutes before slicing to make it a bit easier to cut and serve.

I recommend using the Let's Do Organic brand of finely shredded coconut flakes. This will yield the best texture and result!

KICKING BARBECUE SAUCE

Nut Free, Dairy Free

A bit of sweetness and a bit of heat, this barbecue sauce is full of flavor! I try to keep a batch of this on hand because we love to grill in our house and bottled barbecue sauce is usually filled with sugar.

MAKES ABOUT 2½ CUPS (475 ML)

15 oz (425 ml) tomato sauce

¼ cup (59 ml) molasses*

2 tbsp (24 g) maple sugar

2 tbsp (30 ml) apple cider vinegar

2 tbsp (30 ml) coconut aminos

2 tbsp (30 ml) Dijon mustard

1 tbsp (9 g) tomato paste

1 tsp (5 g) salt

1 tsp (3 g) paprika

½ tsp fresh cracked black pepper

¼-½ tsp cayenne pepper, depending on desired amount of spice

*I usually cut the amount of molasses in half for myself to reduce the amount of sugar.

Place all ingredients in a medium-size saucepan. Whisk together until all ingredients are fully incorporated.

Place a lid on the pot and turn the heat on low. Lightly simmer for 20 minutes, stirring halfway through. Remove the pan from the heat and allow to cool for 30 minutes.

Transfer the barbecue sauce to an airtight container and chill in the refrigerator for a minimum of 2 hours before serving.

Use to garnish any smoked or grilled meat, turn into Pulled Pork Sandwiches (page 102) or add to Pizza (page 186).

SMOKER DRY RUB SEASONING

Nut Free, Dairy Free

This seasoning is the base to most of the smoked meats in this section. Although I usually try
to avoid seasoning main dishes with sugar, the addition of sugar is very important to the smoking process,
because it helps caramelize the outer layer of meat to create the most fabulous texture.

MAKES 1 GENEROUS CUP (240 G)

⅓ cup (67 g) maple sugar

¼ cup (60 g) salt

¼ cup (60 g) black pepper

3 tbsp (26 g) paprika

1½ tsp (5 g) garlic powder

¾ tsp ancho chili powder

½ tsp cayenne pepper

Mix all ingredients together and use as needed to season ribs (page 98) or brisket
(page 108).

Store any leftovers in an airtight container in a cool, dry location for up to 3 months.

SPARKLING LEMONADE

Nut Free, Dairy Free

This sweet and tart lemonade is sweetened with raw honey for a healthy, bubbly drink.
It's the perfect summer drink for all ages!

SERVES 4-6

Honey Simple Syrup

⅓-½ cup (78-118 ml) light-flavored raw honey, depending on desired sweetness

¼ cup (59 ml) water

1 cup (237 ml) fresh-squeezed lemon juice

4-6 cups (947-1420 ml) sparking water, to garnish

To make the simple syrup, pour the water and honey in a small saucepan and whisk together. Lightly heat just until the honey is dissolved, then remove from the heat, allowing it to cool for several minutes.

Mix together the honey simple syrup and fresh lemon juice to create a concentrate.

Fill each cup with ice. Divide the honey lemonade concentrate between the glasses and top with sparkling water, to each person's desired taste.

This & That

Depending on your desired flavor, you can also add frozen fruit such as strawberries, raspberries or mango to the glass to garnish and flavor your lemonade.

When making the honey simple syrup, I often double or triple the recipe to keep it on hand for drink-making.

Old-Fashioned Diner Favorites

Creative Twists on the Timeless Classics

This chapter is filled with classic American food made healthy so that you can enjoy your favorites and still feel great. These recipes are inspired by childhood road trips across Route 66, my grandmother's cooking and, quite often, my daily cravings for comfort food like a hearty burger and fries!

BACON JAM & FRIED EGG BURGERS

Nut Free, Dairy Free, No Added Sugar

Whenever I eat a burger with bacon, the bacon either falls off or I end up eating it first.
So I created this scrumptious onion bacon jam for the perfect bacon taste with each bite. Burgers topped
with a sweet and savory bacon jam and a fried egg—yes, enough said!

MAKES 6 BURGERS

Onion Bacon Jam

½ lb (227 g) bacon

1 medium-size red onion, thinly sliced

4 Medjool dates, pitted

⅓ cup (78 ml) strongly brewed coffee

1 tbsp (15 ml) balsamic vinegar

1 tbsp (15 ml) Dijon mustard

Burgers

2 lbs (907 g) ground beef

Salt and pepper, to taste

6 Burger Buns (page 150)

6 fried eggs with runny yolks

¼ cup (55 g) Duck Fat Mayonnaise
(page 152)

Fresh arugula, for serving

4 oz (114 g) blue cheese (omit for dairy
free)

Warm a large skillet to medium heat. Sear the bacon just until both sides are browned,
but not fully cooked or crispy. Remove the bacon from the pan and set aside.

Sauté the onions in the bacon grease for 5 minutes or until they begin to soften. Add
the bacon, dates, coffee, balsamic vinegar and mustard to the pan and give it a stir.
Place the lid on the pan and reduce the heat to the lowest possible setting.

Cook the bacon jam for 1 hour, stirring once or twice. Add the bacon to the bowl of
a food processor and blend until smooth.

While the jam is cooking, prepare the burgers by warming your grill to medium-high
heat (about 450 to 500°F [232 to 260°C]). Gently form the burgers by shaping into
6 round patties. Season both sides generously with salt and pepper.

Grill the burgers for about 4 minutes, flip and grill an additional 3 to 4 minutes for
medium. Adjust the grilling time based on thickness and your desired serving preference.

While your burgers are grilling, slice the Burger Buns (page 150) in half and lightly
toast them. Warm a large skillet and prepare your fried eggs.

To assemble the burgers, spread a thin layer of mayonnaise on the buns then place the
bottom half of the bun on the plate and layer with a handful of arugula, grilled burger,
blue cheese crumbles, a spoonful of onion bacon jam and a runny yolk fried egg.

This & That

I like to double the bacon jam recipe to keep on hand to accompany a
charcuterie platter or even to eat by the spoonful. It is also delicious when
made into pizza using any of the crusts in this book.

FRIED CHICKEN

Nut Free, Dairy Free, No Added Sugar

One of the most well-known American staples, this fried chicken is great for everyone, from children
to picky eaters or anyone trying to eat healthier. Yes, fried food can be made healthy and tasty too! Fried chicken
is usually made with bone-in chicken, however I chose to use boneless because it can be easily cooked and eaten,
and any leftovers used to make salads or sandwiches. Although it's perfectly crispy and seasoned on its own, my
favorite way is to serve it is with Crispy Bacon Sweet Potato Waffles (page 130) and a drizzle of maple syrup.

SERVES 8

3 lbs (1631 g) boneless, skinless
chicken thighs

1 cup (237 ml) full-fat buttermilk or
1 cup (237 ml) full-fat, unsweetened
coconut milk + 2 tbsp (30 ml) lemon
juice, for dairy free

4 cups (947 ml) coconut oil, tallow or
duck fat, for frying

½ cup (68 g) arrowroot flour

½ cup (68 g) sweet potato starch* or
potato starch

¼ cup (24 g) coconut flour

2¼ tsp (12 g) salt

1½ tsp (4 g) black pepper

1 tsp (3 g) garlic powder

1 tsp (3 g) smoked paprika

½ tsp paprika

¼ tsp cayenne pepper

*See page 242 for explanation

Place the chicken thighs and buttermilk or coconut milk and lemon mixture in a
sealable plastic bag. Use your hands to massage the buttermilk into the chicken and
refrigerate for 6 to 8 hours.

When you are ready to fry your chicken, start by removing it from the refrigerator and
placing it in a strainer to drain out the milk. Allow the chicken to sit for 20 minutes,
giving the strainer a few shakes to remove any excess milk.

Next, warm your oil in a large heavy-bottomed pan or fryer to 350°F (176°C). In a
mixing bowl, sift together your flours and spices, then transfer the flour mixture to a
rimmed baking sheet and spread it out evenly.

Once your oil reaches a steady 350°F (176°C), you are ready to start frying. Dredge
the chicken in the flour, completely covering all sides of the chicken.

Carefully drop the breaded chicken pieces into the hot oil, frying until completely
cooked and golden brown, about 5 to 8 minutes, depending on the size and
thickness of your chicken. Depending on the size of your pan or fryer, you may need
to fry the chicken in batches, because you do not want to overcrowd the pan. If your
chicken is not completely submerged in the oil, simply flip to the other side halfway
through the frying process.

Use tongs to remove the chicken, placing it on a wire rack to drain off any grease.
This also keeps it from getting soggy.

Best served warm and fresh.

CRISPY BACON SWEET POTATO WAFFLES

Dairy Free, No Added Sugar

Savory waffles studded with crispy bacon bits—one of my go-to recipes when wanting a quick alternative to bread. These can be whisked up and enjoyed in just minutes! From breakfast sandwiches to accompanying your Fried Chicken (page 128), these waffles are versatile and delicious.

MAKES 4-5 ROUND WAFFLES

½ cup (68 g) mashed sweet potatoes

1 cup (145 g) raw macadamia nuts

½ cup (118 ml) full-fat, unsweetened coconut milk

2 tbsp (17 g) unsweetened applesauce

3 eggs

2 tbsp (12 g) coconut flour

1 tsp (5 ml) apple cider vinegar

½ tsp baking soda

½ tsp baking powder

6 slices bacon, cooked and crumbled

Coconut oil for greasing waffle iron

To make the mashed sweet potatoes, peel, cube and boil the sweet potatoes for 20 minutes or until tender to touch with a fork. Mash and measure out ½ cup (68 g).

Warm your waffle iron to medium heat. Add all ingredients, except for the bacon, to a high-speed blender and blend for 30 seconds. Scrape down the sides and continue blending for 30 seconds. The batter should be smooth, slightly thick and a very creamy orange color! Finally, stir in the bacon crumbles.

Lightly brush the waffle iron with coconut oil and add a heaping spoonful of batter to the center of the waffle iron, filling it about half full. Cook until your waffle iron signals it is done.

Repeat this process until all the remaining batter is used.

Serve warm topped with butter and maple syrup for something sweet or to accompany Fried Chicken (page 128) for a savory option.

This & That
You can double the batch and freeze any extras. Cool the waffles completely and freeze between layers of parchment paper.

CHOCOLATE COCONUT CREAM PIE

Nut Free, Dairy Free

Nostalgic and homey, but extravagant at the same time, this pie not only is beautiful to make, but each bite reveals a delicious layer of toasted coconut, rich chocolate and luscious coconut cream.

MAKES ONE 9 INCH (22.8 CM) PIE

Toasted Coconut Crust

2 cups (160 g) finely shredded, unsweetened coconut flakes

3 tbsp (44 ml) coconut oil

3 tbsp (44 ml) raw honey

1 tbsp (6 g) + 1 tsp (2 g) coconut flour

1 tsp (5 ml) vanilla extract

Filling

3½ oz (99 g) dark chocolate

1 (13.5 oz [370 ml]) can full-fat, unsweetened coconut milk

1 tsp (3 g) grass-fed gelatin

2 egg yolks

2 tbsp (30 ml) raw honey

1 tsp (5 ml) vanilla extract

½ cup (68 g) finely shredded coconut flakes

16 oz (473 ml) grass-fed heavy cream or coconut cream, whipped

Toasted coconut and chocolate shavings, for garnish

Add all the crust ingredients to the bowl of a food processor and pulse several times until the coconut is mixed and crumbly.

Spoon the coconut mixture into a 9 inch (22.8 cm) tart pan with a removable bottom (if your pan is not nonstick, you will need to brush it with coconut oil). Use a small spatula or the tips of your fingers to evenly and firmly press into the bottom and sides of the tart pan. Be patient with the process because it is what makes the crust stick together.

Bake for 9 to 12 minutes or until the crust is golden brown. Set aside to cool for 10 minutes.

To make the filling, melt the chocolate over low heat in a saucepan. Spoon the melted chocolate into the bottom of the pie crust, spreading evenly around the cooled crust.

Add the coconut milk to a saucepan and sprinkle the gelatin on top. Set it aside to bloom for 10 minutes. Whisk together the egg yolks, honey and vanilla. Heat the pan on low, stirring until the gelatin dissolves. Add in the egg yolk mixture and continue stirring and heating for about 15 minutes or until the milk starts to steam. Stir in the shredded coconut flakes. Set it aside to cool for 30 minutes.

Carefully and slowly pour the cooled milk over the crust. Lightly cover the pie and chill in the refrigerator for 4 hours.

To make homemade whipped coconut cream, place 2 (13.5 oz [370 ml]) cans full-fat, unsweetend coconut milk in the refrigerator for a minimum of 24 hours. Carefully remove the lid and scrape off the top layer of cream that has risen to the top. Discard or save the coconut water. Use beaters or a hand mixer to whip the cream until soft, foamy peaks form.

Top with whipped cream, toasted coconut and chocolate shavings.

Slice and serve!

This & That

The secret to creating each perfect layer of this pie is to allow the crust, chocolate and milk to cool before adding the next layer, otherwise they will come together as one messy layer rather than stay separated.

Due to the nature of coconut and coconut oil, the crust will crumble slightly when at room temperature. I recommend removing from the refrigerator 5 minutes prior to slicing.

SMOKY CHIPOTLE BACON STUFFED BURGERS WITH GRILLED PINEAPPLE

Nut Free, Dairy Free

I am truly the girl who thinks burgers are a food group of their own, and I never grow tired of eating them! Flavors and toppings are endless, but these 50-50-50 burgers stuffed with bacon are magical. The smoky and spicy chipotle mayonnaise blends nicely with the sweet pineapple.

MAKES 6 BURGERS

½ cup (110 g) Duck Fat Mayonnaise (page 152)

1½ tsp (5 g) chipotle chili powder

¼ tsp maple sugar

½ lb (227 g) bacon

1 lb (454 g) ground beef

1 lb (454 g) ground pork

Salt and pepper, to taste

6 slices pineapple, cored and about ½-inch (1.3-cm) thick

6 Burger Buns (page 150), sliced and toasted

Lettuce leaves, for serving

Warm the barbecue to medium-high heat (about 450 to 500°F [232 to 260°C]). Stir together the mayonnaise, chipotle and maple sugar. Set aside in the refrigerator until needed.

Use a sharp knife to cut the bacon into very small pieces. Mix together the ground beef, pork and bacon until incorporated, being careful not to overmix or the meat will become gummy. Divide the meat into six equal sections, shaping into flat round patties.

Generously season both sides with salt and pepper, patting the seasoning into the meat with your fingers.

Grill the pineapple slices for 2 minutes, flip to the other side and cook for an additional 2 minutes. Next, grill the burgers for 4 to 5 minutes, flip to the other side and cook for an additional 4 to 5 minutes. The grill time really depends on how thick you make your burgers and your heat temperature, but keep in mind that these beef and pork burgers take a bit longer to cook than beef burgers.

Serve the burgers with buns, layering first a lettuce leaf, slice of pineapple, grilled burger patties and a drizzle of chipotle mayonnaise.

This & That

If you want the best-tasting burgers, I recommend using natural fire from real firewood.

CREAMY COFFEE ICE CREAM

Nut Free, Dairy Free

Coffee ice cream has forever been my favorite flavor.
I remember licking a coffee-ice-cream-filled cone on many warm summer nights!
Because of the small amount of alcohol, this ice cream will not become hard and icy after freezing!
Serve a scoop on top of my warm Double Chocolate Fudge Brownies (page 170).

SERVES 6

2 cups (473 ml) full-fat, unsweetened coconut milk

½ cup (118 ml) coconut cream or heavy whipping cream

¼ cup (59 ml) raw honey

3 egg yolks

2 tbsp (30 ml) fresh, finely ground dark roasted coffee

¼ cup (60 ml) Kahlua coffee liqueur

Whisk together the milk, cream, honey, yolks and ground coffee. Pour the batter into a saucepan and warm to medium-low heat.

Heat the batter just until the milk begins to steam, stirring occasionally so the milk does not burn. This should take about 15 minutes or until the milk comes to a temperature of 175°F (79°C). Remove from the heat and whisk in the Kahlua liqueur.

Allow the batter to cool for 15 minutes before transferring to the refrigerator. Chill for a minimum of 4 hours.

Churn in an ice cream maker according to the manufacturer's instructions. For best results, place in the freezer for 20 minutes after churning.

Enjoy a scoop or two.

This & That

The addition of alcohol helps retain ice cream's desired creamy consistency even after freezing. Alcohol has a low freezing point and is a great way to soften ice cream. Only a small amount of alcohol is used, and most of it is cooked out, so go ahead and enjoy!

ONION RINGS

Nut Free, Dairy Free, No Added Sugar

The origins of onion rings are subject to debate, but most of us will remember them from old-fashioned diners or fast-food restaurants. They're great as a crunchy appetizer or served as a side with burgers.
Feel free to dip them in any of your favorite sauces.

SERVES 6

4 cups (950 ml) coconut oil, duck fat or tallow, for frying

1 large white onion

¾ cup (102 g) + 2 tbsp (17 g) arrowroot flour

1½ tbsp (9 g) coconut flour

1 tsp (5 g) salt

½ tsp garlic powder

¼ tsp paprika

⅛ tsp cayenne pepper

2 eggs

2 tbsp (30 ml) full-fat, unsweetened coconut milk

Kicking Barbeue Sauce (page 118), for serving

In a large heavy-bottomed pan or fryer, slowly heat your oil to 350°F (176°C). You will want 2 to 3 inches (5 to 7.6 cm) of oil in order to fry the onion rings.

Cut the onion into ½-inch (1.2-cm)-thick slices, separating into individual rings.

Sift together all dry ingredients. Add in the eggs and coconut milk, whisking together until smooth. Allow the batter to sit for 1 minute then whisk together again.

Once your oil is hot, dip each individual onion ring into the batter. Working in batches so you do not overcrowd the pan, drop the battered onion rings into the oil, frying for 4 to 5 minutes or just until they start to turn golden brown. Remove the rings with tongs, placing on a wire rack to prevent from getting soggy. Repeat this process until you have fried all the onion rings.

Serve with Kicking Barbecue Sauce or your favorite type of mustard.

This & That

Keep in mind that these will be a bit lighter in color than the beer-battered onion rings that are most common in restaurants.

DUCK FAT FRIES—HAVE THEM YOUR WAY

Nut Free, Dairy Free, No Added Sugar

There is nothing more comforting than old-fashioned fries, and I occasionally eat white potatoes, especially when fried in duck fat. The flavor and texture is simply incredible. Everyone likes their fries seasoned differently, so I created a few different versions so that you can have them your way. If you are cooking for a large crowd, you can make the fries and set out all the seasonings; that way each person can flavor their own.

SERVES 4-6

Classic French Fries

3 large russet potatoes

4 cups (946 ml) duck fat

Sea salt to taste

Cajun Seasoning Mix

1 tbsp (15 g) salt

1½ tsp (5 g) garlic powder

1½ tsp (5 g) smoked paprika

½ tsp black pepper

½ tsp onion powder

¼ tsp dried thyme

¼ tsp cayenne pepper

Rosemary, Garlic Truffle Seasoning

2 tbsp (30 ml) truffle oil

2 cloves garlic, crushed

1 tsp (3 g) fresh rosemary, chopped

Slice the potatoes into ½-inch (1.2-cm)-thick slices. Place the potatoes in a large bowl and cover with ice water. Set aside for 30 minutes. Strain the potatoes, patting dry with paper towels.

If using the Cajun or rosemary, garlic truffle seasoning, mix together the seasoning ingredients (if using the Cajun seasoning, keep in mind you will have plenty extra).

In a large heavy-bottomed pan or fryer, slowly heat the duck fat to 325°F (162°C).

Working in batches, carefully drop the potatoes into the hot oil and fry for 5 to 7 minutes or until light golden brown, depending on the thickness of your fries. Remove the fries with tongs, draining any excess grease, and set on a wire rack. Repeat with the remaining potatoes until you have partially cooked all fries.

Next, raise your frying heat to 375°F (191°C), giving it several minutes to come to a stable temperature.

Working in batches, add the partially cooked potatoes back into the hot oil, cooking for 1 to 2 minutes, depending on your thickness and desired end texture, or until a rich golden brown color.

As each batch comes out of the frying pan, and while they are still warm, season the fries with your desired flavorings. Repeat with remaining fries.

Best served fresh and warm.

BREAKFAST FOR DINNER CHEESY "GRITS"

Nut Free, Dairy Free, No Added Sugar

Since breakfast is my favorite meal of the day, I am always looking for any excuse to enjoy eggs and bacon for any meal. These "grits" are made entirely from vegetables, and they're the perfect comfort food. You can serve this as a side dish to any meal or top with a runny, poached egg as pictured.

SERVES 4

---

1 large head cauliflower

4 tbsp (58 g) butter or ghee*

2 cloves garlic, crushed

1 tsp (5 g) salt

2 tbsp (30 ml) coconut milk or grass-fed heavy cream

6 oz (170 g) sharp cheddar cheese, shredded*

Fresh cracked black pepper, to taste

Poached eggs and bacon for serving

*For dairy-free, substitute the butter with bacon grease, and the cheese with 1 teaspoon (5 g) nutritional yeast and 1 tablespoon (15 g) arrowroot flour.

Slice the cauliflower into small florets, discarding the outer leaves and inner core. Using the grating attachment of a food processor, "rice" the cauliflower florets.

Warm a deep pan over low heat and melt the butter. Sauté in the garlic and salt until it starts to become fragrant. Mix in the cauliflower and milk, stirring until combined (if making this dairy-free, add the arrowroot flour). Heat for 20 minutes or until the cauliflower is very soft, stirring occasionally.

Turn the heat off and stir in the shredded cheese or nutritional yeast. Place a lid on top of the skillet and set aside for 5 minutes. Stir one last time just before serving. Serve, topped with fresh cracked black pepper and poached eggs or bacon.

This & That

See directions for poaching eggs on page 42.

SALTED CARAMEL ICE CREAM SUNDAES

Nut Free

Creamy vanilla ice cream drizzled with sweet caramel sauce for a slightly sweet and salty combination. Once you have made up a batch of both the sauce and the ice cream, your serving possibilities are endless, so go ahead and scoop and drizzle away. My favorite way to serve is to create banana splits or make warm brownies (page 170), Banana Bread Waffles (page 22) or Apple Pie (page 200) à la mode!

SERVES 6

Vanilla Ice Cream

2 cups (474 ml) full-fat, unsweetened coconut milk

½ cup (118 ml) coconut cream

½ cup (68 ml) maple syrup

3 egg yolks

2 tsp (10 ml) vanilla extract

Salted Caramel Sauce

4 tbsp (58 g) butter or ghee

½ cup (118 ml) raw honey

½ cup (118 ml) full-fat, unsweetened coconut milk

½ tsp vanilla extract

¼ tsp sea salt

First, start by preparing the vanilla ice cream. Add the coconut milk, cream, maple syrup and egg yolks to a blender. Blend on high for 20 seconds or until completely smooth.

Pour the milk mixture into a saucepan and heat over low for 10 to15 minutes or until the milk begins to steam. Be sure to stir occasionally so that the milk does not burn.

Remove the pan from the heat and stir in the vanilla extract. Set aside to cool for 15 minutes before transferring to the refrigerator to cool completely for a minimum of 4 hours.

Churn in an ice cream maker according to the manufacturer's instructions. For best results, transfer the churned ice cream to the freezer to chill for 20 minutes before serving.

While the ice cream is chilling and churning, begin to make the caramel sauce. Over low heat, melt the butter. Add in the raw honey and coconut milk, stirring in the same direction for 30 seconds.

Turn the heat up to medium until the sauce begins to gently boil. Allow it to continue gently boiling, untouched, for 10 minutes, being careful as it may splatter a bit.

Remove the pan from the heat and stir in the vanilla and salt. Set the caramel aside to cool for 30 minutes, allowing it to thicken.

Serve a drizzle over vanilla ice cream or with a slice of warm Apple Pie (page 200), making it à la mode.

Any remaining sauce can be stored in the refrigerator, lightly warming it as needed.

This & That

Please note, this is not a thick caramel sauce. I wanted it to be thin enough to drizzle over ice cream without it quickly hardening.

FRIED EGG BLT SANDWICH

Nut Free, Dairy Free, No Added Sugar

This is the classic bacon, lettuce and tomato sandwich with the added goodness of a fried egg and avocado.
I usually keep a few slices of Nut-Free Sandwich Bread (page 30) in the freezer to whisk up
a comfort food meal in a matter of minutes!

MAKES 2 SANDWICHES

6 slices bacon

4 slices Nut-Free Sandwich Bread
(page 30)

2 eggs

2 tbsp (30 ml) Ranch Dressing
(page 168)

Lettuce leaves

1 small tomato, sliced

½ avocado, sliced

Warm a large skillet to medium heat. Cook the bacon slices until crispy. Set them aside on a paper towel.

Lightly toast your bread so that it is warm with slightly crispy edges.

Next, fry the eggs in the bacon grease until cooked to desired preference, although slightly runny yolks are best.

Cut your bread in half and spread both sides with ranch dressing. Add lettuce and tomato slices to the one half of the bread, then layer on the bacon, fried egg and avocado slices. Top with the other half of the bread.

BUILD YOUR OWN MILKSHAKES

Nut Free, Dairy Free

Nothing says American food quite like a good burger finished off with a creamy, sweet milkshake. With just a few ingredient swaps, these milkshakes can be made in the comfort of your own home without all the added sugars. My favorite is the The Elvis, named after the singer's love of bananas, peanut butter and bacon. Be sure to dip your crispy bacon slices in the rich milkshake—it is delicious!

EACH MILKSHAKE SERVES 2-3

The Elvis

3 bananas, peeled, sliced and frozen

½ cup (118 ml) full-fat, unsweetened coconut milk

¼ cup (34 g) sunflower seed butter

½ tsp (3 ml) vanilla extract

6 slices cooked bacon, to garnish

Whipped cream to garnish, optional

Strawberries and Cream

1 cup (136 g) frozen strawberries, heaping full

1 cup (68 g) Vanilla Ice Cream (page 144)

½ cup (118 ml) full-fat, unsweetened coconut milk

Fresh strawberries to garnish, optional

Whipped cream to garnish, optional

Java Chip

2 cups (272 g) Creamy Coffee Ice Cream (page 136)

½ cup (118 ml) full-fat, unsweetened coconut milk

¼ cup (34 g) chocolate chips or chunks

Whipped cream to garnish, optional

Depending on what milkshake you are making, place all ingredients, with the exception of the garnish ingredients, in a blender. Blend for 10 to 20 seconds, depending on the strength of your blender, or until the milkshake is smooth and creamy but still thick.

Pour into desired amount of glasses and garnish with your chosen toppings.

BURGER BUNS OR SANDWICH ROLLS

Dairy Free, No Added Sugar

Although I have grown fond of eating my burger without a bun, there is something about a warm, slightly crusty bun to stuff full of your favorite flavors. This recipe is based on a popular recipe for fluffy, white rolls on my blog, Colorful Eats, but I re-created them using ingredients that are more practical to find. They stay together fabulously, even when filled, and I use them for everything from burgers to sandwiches to just toasted with a bit of butter. I usually freeze extras to keep on hand when craving some comfort food!

MAKES 8 BUNS

Coconut oil, for brushing tins

2 cups (290 g) raw cashew pieces

2 tbsp (29 g) butter or ghee*, melted

5 eggs

2 tbsp (30 ml) full-fat, unsweetened coconut milk

¼ cup (34 g) arrowroot flour

¼ cup (25 g) coconut flour

1 tsp (4 g) baking soda

¼ tsp baking powder

¼ tsp salt

1 tbsp (15 ml) apple cider vinegar

½ tsp sesame seeds, to garnish

½ tsp poppy seeds, to garnish

Use coconut oil for strict dairy free.

Preheat the oven to 340°F (171°C), adjusting the rack to the middle position. Generously brush 8 (3 inch [7.6 cm]) round English muffin rings with coconut oil and place them on a parchment-lined baking tray.

Add the cashew pieces to the bowl of a food processor and blend the nuts for 1 minute, then scrape down the sides and bottom with a spatula. Add in the melted butter and blend for an additional minute; at this point the cashews should resemble a smooth nut butter. Scrape down the sides and bottom once again.

Add the eggs, coconut milk, arrowroot flour, coconut flour, baking soda, baking powder and salt. Briefly blend until smooth, then scrape down the sides and bottom. Finally, add the apple cider vinegar and blend one last time.

Immediately pour the batter into the prepared rings, filling each ring halfway.

Sprinkle with sesame and poppy seeds just before placing them into the oven.

Bake for 16 to 18 minutes or until a tester comes out clean, watching carefully at the end because you do not want to overcook them.

Allow the buns to cool for 5 minutes before pushing them up from the bottom to remove the rings. If your buns are sticking slightly, just run a knife along the edges of the rings first.

Serve with your favorite burger or sandwich fillings!

This & That

I decided to use cashew pieces because they are generally less expensive. Substituting whole cashews will work, but you will need to weigh them to match the correct amount.

To make a nut free version, use the batter from Nut-Free Sandwich Bread (page 30) in 6 greased muffin rings. Bake at 350°F (176°C) for 21–23 minutes.

DUCK FAT MAYONNAISE

Nut Free, Dairy Free, No Added Sugar

I had never been a fan of mayonnaise until I created this Paleo version using a combination of duck fat and olive oil. It took me countless tries to finally get this recipe right, but this smooth and creamy version is simply delightful! Word of advice—be very patient making this, but I promise the technique is flawless.

MAKES ABOUT 1½ CUPS (330 G)

2 eggs

5 tsp (25 ml) apple cider vinegar

½ cup (118 ml) rendered duck fat, liquid but not hot

½ cup (110 ml) light-tasting olive oil

½ tsp Dijon mustard

¼ tsp salt

Crack the eggs into a blender and add the apple cider vinegar. Place the lid on the blender and set aside to come to room temperature for 1 hour.

Add the duck fat and olive oil to a measuring cup—something with a small spout so that it can be poured easily—and whisk together.

After 1 hour, blend the eggs and vinegar on high for 60 seconds. With the blender still running on high, slowly add the fat, starting with a drop or two then working up to a very slow and steady drizzle. This entire process should take 5 to 8 minutes, so yes, be patient, but the result is worth it! Finally, add the mustard and salt, and blend for an additional 30 seconds.

At this point, your mayonnaise should be warm, due to the blender running for so long, and it will resemble mayonnaise, but it will still be a little runny. Refrigerate the mayonnaise for 1 hour, then stir again and use as needed.

Store any extra mayonnaise in the refrigerator for 1 to 2 weeks.

Game-Day Eats

Party Bites and Nibbles to Cheer on Your Team

The hardest time for me to stay true to a healthy way of eating is when I am surrounded by junk food or offered something I can't eat at a party. This chapter is designed to make football tailgates or game-watching days tasty and enjoyable once again, allowing you to have something to munch on as you gather with friends! These recipes are great for any gathering, party or just everyday life.

SMOKED CHICKEN WINGS

Nut Free, Dairy Free

Traditional wings are breaded and fried, but these wings are slowly smoked over fire, allowing them
to be tender and flavorful. You can start smoking them just before guests begin to arrive,
and enjoy the smoky aroma all day long.

MAKES ABOUT 20 INDIVIDUAL WINGS

2 lbs (907 g) chicken wings

1 tbsp (15 ml) olive oil

2 tbsp (17 g) smoker seasoning
(page 120)

Prepare your smoker with hickory wood, bringing the fire to a constant temperature
of 225°F (107°C).

Use kitchen shears to separate the wing and the drumette at the joint into two pieces.
(If you have never done this before, it can be a bit tricky at first, but after separating
a few wings you will get the hang of it.)

Toss the wings with olive oil, then sprinkle both sides generously with seasoning.

Place the wings on the grill grates. Smoke for about 1½ to 2 hours or until the
chicken comes to an internal temperature of 165°F (73°C). Maintain the fire, adding
fuel when necessary to prevent the temperature from dropping too low.

Serve with a side of Ranch Dressing (page 168) and vegetable sticks, if desired.

This & That

Like any cut of meat, chicken wings can vary greatly in size, so be sure to
trust the internal temperature of the meat, not the suggested cooking times.

LOADED NACHOS

Nut Free, Dairy Free, No Added Sugar

Taro chips are made from the root vegetable dasheen and have a crunchy texture and mild taste,
making them perfect for nachos. The secret to nachos is making each chip its own masterpiece of toppings,
so that no person experiences that sad moment of reaching for an empty chip. Pile these grain-free nachos
high with your favorite toppings and feel free to substitute Chorizo (page 20) or Carnitas (page 66)
for the meat if you have it on hand.

SERVES 3-4

---

1 lb (454 g) ground beef

½ small red onion, minced

½ cup (68 g) sweet red bell pepper, minced

2 tbsp (17 g) tomato paste

1 tsp (3 g) ancho chili powder

1 tsp (3 g) ground cumin

½ tsp salt

½ tsp garlic powder

⅛ tsp black pepper

Dash of cayenne pepper, to taste

6 oz (170 g) taro chips

8 oz (227 g) sharp cheddar cheese, grated (omit for dairy free)

Pico De Gallo

1 lb (454 g) fresh tomatoes

½ fresh jalapeño, stem and seeds removed

½ cup (68 g) fresh cilantro, about 2 handfuls

¼ red onion

1 lime, juiced

1 clove garlic, crushed

Pinch of salt

Garnish Suggestions

Avocado slices

Guacamole (page 164)

Black olives

Hot sauce

Thinly sliced lettuce

Lime wedges

Warm a large skillet to medium heat. Preheat the oven to 350°F (176°C). Line a large, rimmed baking sheet with parchment paper and set aside.

Brown the ground beef in the skillet, crumbling the meat into small pieces. After about 3 minutes, once the meat is partially cooked, drain out any excess grease. Add in the onions, bell peppers, tomato paste and all spices. Lightly simmer for 15 minutes, stirring occasionally.

Lay the chips out on the baking sheet, creating an even layer with not too many chips piled on top of each other. Top with the taco meat and shredded cheese.

Bake for 7 to 10 minutes or until the cheese is fully melted and bubbly.

While the nachos are baking, make the pico de gallo by finely chopping all ingredients and stirring together.

Top the nachos with pico de gallo and any other desired toppings.

This & That

To make dairy free, omit the cheese and skip the step where you cook the nachos in the oven.

Of all the root vegetable chips, I think taro has the mildest taste, but feel free to make these with sweet potato or plantain chips if that is what you have on hand.

CHEDDAR CHORIZO DIP

Nut Free, No Added Sugar

This is a favorite dish in our household, one that always seems to be eaten instantly! Most cheese-style dips you will find are made with processed cheese and are full of questionable ingredients, so I wanted to make this yummy party appetizer using real, natural ingredients. If you cannot tolerate dairy, I sincerely apologize in advance, but for those of you who can, dig in and enjoy! I like to serve this with sweet potato or root vegetable chips or, if you are anything like me, you will just eat it by the spoonful!

SERVES 6-8

1 tsp (5 ml) olive oil

½ large red onion, thinly sliced

½ batch (or 1 lb [454 g]) Mexican Chorizo Sausage, uncooked (page 20)

8 oz (227 g) full-fat cream cheese

8 oz (227 g) cheddar cheese, shredded and divided in half

Preheat the oven to 350°F (176°C) and warm an 8 inch (20.3 cm) skillet with the olive oil to medium-low heat.

Sauté the onions for 20 minutes or until they are soft. Transfer the onions to a mixing bowl and set aside.

Turn up the heat to medium. Brown and crumble the chorizo sausage until it is browned on all sides. Add the sausage crumbles to the mixing bowl along with the cream cheese and half of the cheddar cheese. Stir the mixture until it is completely mixed, then transfer it back into the skillet. Sprinkle the remaining cheese on top, completely covering the top.

Bake for 25 to 30 minutes or until the top of the cheese starts to bubble and turn golden brown.

Serve warm with root vegetable chips or even by the spoonful!

PIGS IN A BLANKET

Nut Free, Dairy Free, No Sugar Added

Simple and completely delicious, this game-day finger food really needs no explanation.
No matter how you or your guests may eat…everyone loves bacon!

MAKES 18 BITE-SIZE APPETIZERS

6 all-natural beef hot dogs, preferably sugar free

9 slices bacon

Toothpicks, for assembling and serving

Preheat the oven to 375°F (190°C).

Slice the hot dogs into thirds and the bacon slices in half.

Tightly wrap each hot dog with a bacon slice, pinning down the ends with a toothpick if desired.

Place on a baking sheet. Repeat this process until you have used up all the ingredients.

Bake for 30 minutes or until your bacon is golden brown and cooked.

Cool for 5 minutes before serving with your favorite sauce—mustard or Kicking Barbecue Sauce (page 118).

This & That

Both US Wellness Meats and Applegate have all-natural and sugar-free beef hot dogs. Some brands are thicker than others, so adjust the amount of bacon needed based on the size of your hot dogs.

SHREDDED CHICKEN ENCHILADA GUACAMOLE BURGERS

Nut Free, Dairy Free, No Added Sugar

My husband absolutely loves enchiladas, so after searching in vain for a red sauce I felt comfortable using,
I decided to invent my own. I created this as a simple dish to prepare for any festivity—it is great for potluck
situations or to allow people to garnish how they please. My grain-free spin on classic enchiladas
is transforming them into burgers, piled with smoky shredded chicken and scoops of fresh guacamole.
Keep in mind this is a messy dish, but dig in, enjoy and keep the napkins handy!

SERVES 6

---

1 cup (236 ml) tomato sauce

1 tsp (5 ml) apple cider vinegar

1½ tsp (4 g) ancho chili powder

1 tsp (3 g) garlic powder

½ tsp chipotle chili powder

¾ tsp salt

2 tbsp (30 ml) olive oil, divided

¼ cup (34 g) red onion, minced

1½ lbs (681 g) chicken breasts

2 poblano or pasilla peppers

Olive oil and salt for roasting peppers

6 Burger Buns or Sandwich Rolls
(page 150), for serving

6 slices raw sharp cheddar cheese,
optional (omit for dairy free)

Guacamole

3 ripe Hass avocados

2 tbsp (17 g) fresh cilantro, finely
chopped

2 tbsp (17 g) red onion, minced

2 tbsp (30 ml) fresh lime juice or about
1 lime juiced

½ tsp salt

½ tsp garlic powder

Fresh cracked black pepper, to taste

Preheat the oven to 325°F (162°C) and warm a Dutch oven to medium heat on the stove.

In a mixing bowl, stir together the tomato sauce, apple cider vinegar, spices and salt and set aside.

Add 1 tablespoon (15 ml) olive oil to the warm pan and sauté the onions for 5 minutes or until they start to soften. Remove the onions from the pan, adding them to the tomato sauce mixture, and set aside.

Next add the remaining tablespoon (15 ml) of olive oil to the pan. Sear the chicken for 2 minutes, rotate to the other side and sear for an additional 2 minutes. Pour the tomato sauce mixture over the chicken and place a lid on top of the pan. Place in the oven and bake the chicken for 35 to 40 minutes, depending on the thickness of the breast meat. Use two forks to shred the chicken apart in the pan, allowing it to soak up the juices.

Turn the oven temperature up to 400°F (204°C). Slice the stems off the peppers, remove and discard the inner seeds. Slice the peppers into thin strips and place on a baking sheet, tossing lightly with a bit of olive oil and pinch of salt. Roast for 20 minutes.

Prepare the guacamole by peeling the avocados and discarding the pits. Mash the avocados together and mix in the seasonings.

To assemble, slice the rolls in half, laying a slice of cheese on the bottom half (optional, omit for dairy free). Toast the rolls until the cheese is melted. Add a scoop of shredded chicken, then roasted poblano peppers and finally garnish with guacamole.

Serve and enjoy!

This & That
The shredded chicken enchilada meat is delicious on top of Loaded Nachos (page 158) or served with Soft Plantain Tortillas (page 84), so feel free to double the chicken recipe to keep it on hand and use in your favorite Mexican dishes.

BUFFALO CHICKEN MEATBALLS

Dairy Free, No Added Sugar

A creative twist on the classic buffalo chicken wings, made into meatballs instead! These are perfect for game-day festivities because you can wrap them in foil and keep them warm until you are ready to eat. They're packed with flavor and a bit of heat, and I usually serve them over a bed of arugula with blue cheese crumbles or Creamy Ranch Dressing (page 168).

MAKES 16 MEATBALLS

1 cup (110 g) almond flour

2 tsp (10 g) salt

2 tsp (6 g) garlic powder

2 lbs (907 g) ground chicken

⅓ cup (45 g) green onions, chopped

2 tbsp (30 ml) olive oil, for searing

⅔ cup (158 ml) buffalo hot sauce*

2 handfuls fresh arugula leaves

4 oz (113 g) blue cheese crumbles, optional (omit for dairy free)

Coconut oil for greasing hands

Ranch Dressing (page 168), for serving

I use Frank's hot sauce.

Preheat the oven to 350°F (176°C) and warm a large nonstick skillet to medium heat.

In the bottom of a mixing bowl, sift together the almond flour, salt and garlic. Add in the ground chicken and green onions. Use your hands to mix together the meat, incorporating all the ingredients, but be careful not to overmix because the chicken will become gummy.

Lightly grease your hands with coconut oil, shape the chicken into small meatballs and set them aside on a plate. If the chicken becomes too difficult to work with, wash and re-grease your hands.

Drizzle the olive oil in the warm skillet, swirling around to coat all sides of the skillet. Sear the meatballs for 8 minutes, rotating every 2 minutes so that all sides are seared.

Transfer the meatballs to a baking dish, placing them close together so that all sides are touching. This is easiest if the baking dish is similar in size to the meatballs; I find that a 9 by 13 inch (22.8 by 33 cm) dish usually works well. Pour the hot sauce over the meatballs and place in the oven.

Bake for 20 minutes.

Serve over a bed of arugula with blue cheese crumbles or Ranch Dressing.

This & That
If you cannot find ground chicken, most butchers will freshly grind chicken thighs for you. Just ask!

DOUBLE CHOCOLATE FUDGE BROWNIES

Dairy Free

If grain-free baking intimidates you, start with these brownies. They are simple to make and a great way to introduce yourself and your loved ones to healthy desserts. With the addition of chocolate chunks, you will get the perfect gooey, chocolaty taste with every bite. These brownies are delicious by themselves, but even better with a scoop of Creamy Coffee Ice Cream (page 136) on top!

MAKES 9 MEDIUM-SIZE SQUARE BROWNIES

Coconut oil, for brushing pan

1 cup (136 g) creamy almond butter

⅓ cup (79 ml) maple syrup

3 eggs

½ cup (40 g) raw cacao powder

½ cup (118 ml) full-fat, unsweetened coconut milk

1 tsp (5 ml) vanilla extract

¾ tsp baking soda

Pinch of salt

3½ oz (99 g) dark chocolate bar, chopped*

*I recommend using Pure 7 chocolate bars because they are minimally sweetened with raw honey.

Preheat the oven to 350°F (176°C). Brush the bottom and sides of an 8 by 8 inch (20.3 by 20.3 cm) pan with coconut oil and set aside.

In a bowl, blend together the almond butter, syrup, eggs, cacao powder, coconut milk, vanilla extract, baking soda and salt. Scrape down the sides and bottom of the bowl and blend again. Fold in the chocolate chunks.

Pour the batter into the pan and bake for 25 to 27 minutes or until a tester comes out clean. Keep in mind that you want the center slightly gooey, because it will continue to cook out of the oven.

Cool for 5 to 10 minutes before slicing.

CHILI TO SHARE WITH ALL THE FIXINGS

Nut Free, Dairy Free, No Added Sugar

This chili is spiced and hearty, full of flavor and ready to be shared on a chilly day! Traditional chili is packed with beans, so instead, I added roasted sweet potatoes for some texture. I love to add chicharrones, which remind me of corn chips, for a bit of crunch on top. Grab a bowl and pile on your favorite toppings!

SERVES 8

2 dried New Mexico chilis

2 dried chipotle chilis

1 lb (454 g) ground beef

1 lb (454 g) ground pork

1 sweet red bell pepper, minced

½ large red onion, minced

3 large cloves garlic, crushed

2½ tsp (13 g) salt

1 tsp (3 g) cumin

½ tsp smoked paprika

¾ cup (177 ml) chicken or beef broth

1 (15 oz [425 g]) can tomato sauce

1 (14.5 oz [411 g]) can fire-roasted diced tomatoes

½ lime, juiced

1 large sweet potato

2 tsp (10 ml) olive oil

All the Fixings

Chicharrones (fried pork rinds)

Green onions

Cilantro

Avocado slices

Sour cream

Cheddar cheese

Snip the ends off the chilis and scrape out the inside seeds. Place the chilis in a blender and cover with hot water, then set aside for 20 minutes to soften.

While you are waiting, heat a large soup pot to medium heat. Sear the ground beef and pork, browning and crumbling, but do not worry about fully cooking the meat. Remove with a slotted spoon and set aside.

In the leftover meat juices, sauté the red bell pepper, onion, garlic, salt, cumin and smoked paprika for 5 minutes or until the onions start to soften and become fragrant.

Now strain the water out of the blender and add the broth. Blend on high for 60 seconds or until the chilis are completely blended and the mixture is a deep red color.

Reduce the pan heat to the lowest possible setting and add in the browned meat, chili and broth liquid mixture, tomato sauce, diced tomatoes and lime juice. Stir to mix, then place the lid on the pot and simmer for 1 to 1½ hours.

Meanwhile, roast the sweet potatoes and prepare any desired toppings in small bowls for serving. Warm the oven to 400°F (204°C). Slice the sweet potatoes into small cubes about ½ inch (1.2 cm) thick. Toss them with the olive oil and roast for 35 minutes, stirring halfway through.

Just before serving, stir in the roasted sweet potatoes. Serve warm with any desired toppings.

COCONUT FRIED SHRIMP
WITH MANGO HABANERO DIPPING SAUCE

Nut Free, Dairy Free, No Added Sugar

Fried shrimp with a crunchy coconut shell, this is a great appetizer to serve at any party.
It's a crowd pleaser, and comes together in just minutes.

SERVES 3-4

Coconut Fried Shrimp

4 cups (946 ml) coconut oil, for frying shrimp

2 eggs, whisked

1½ cups (120 g) finely shredded unsweetened coconut flakes

½ cup (68 g) arrowroot flour

1½ tsp (8 g) salt

1 tsp (3 g) garlic powder

½ tsp onion powder

¼ tsp paprika

¼ tsp black pepper

1 lb (454 g) fresh jumbo shrimp or tiger prawns, deveined, shells and tails removed

Mango Habanero Dipping Sauce

1 mango

1 habanero pepper

2 tbsp (17 g) Duck Fat Mayonnaise (page 152)

½ lime, juiced

In a heavy-bottomed pan or fryer, slowly heat the oil to 350°F (176°C), allowing for 2 to 3 inches of oil to fry the shrimp.

Make the mango habanero dipping sauce by adding all the ingredients to a blender and blending on high until smooth. Pour the sauce into a bowl and set aside.

In one bowl, whisk together the eggs until smooth. In a shallow bowl, mix together the coconut flakes, arrowroot flour and spices.

Dip the shrimp into the egg batter, then in the coconut mixture, evenly coating all sides. Place the shrimp on a plate and repeat this process with the remaining shrimp.

Keeping the oil temperature steady and working in batches, fry the shrimp for 2½ to 3 minutes, depending on the size of your shrimp, or until they are golden brown. You do not want to overcrowd the pan or the shrimp will not fry properly. Remove the shrimp from the oil and place on a wire rack so that they do not become soggy. Repeat this process until all shrimp are fried.

Best served warm with the mango habanero dipping sauce.

This & That

Fried shrimp usually has the tail intact, but since this is a party appetizer, I recommend removing the tail so that guests have less trash to keep in hand.

Movie Night

Family Favorites for the Kids at Heart

Although I do not yet have children of my own, these recipes are largely inspired by my childhood favorites, and I hope one day, my children grow to love them too. This chapter contains some of my favorites, because I always say I am just a kid at heart. Many of these recipes give you the flexibility of allowing each person to pick his or her own flavors, like pizza toppings, for example. Having the whole family involved in the cooking process makes it memorable and tasty, too!

HOT DOGS ON A STICK

Dairy Free, No Added Sugar

I always remember shopping for school clothes in the fall, and my mom allowing my sister and
me to get a treat at the mall food court. I always chose a hot dog on a stick with French fries.
I am honestly such a kid at heart, and this is one of my all-time-favorite recipes in the book! It is a great way
to get the little ones, or adults like me, involved in the cooking process and re-create this
classic childhood favorite using healthy ingredients.

MAKES 6 HOT DOGS OR 12 MINI ONES, AS PICTURED

---

4 cups (946 ml) coconut oil, tallow or
duck fat for frying

¾ cup (108 g) raw cashew pieces

½ cup (68 g) arrowroot flour

1 tbsp (6 g) coconut flour

½ tsp baking powder

½ tsp salt

3 eggs

12 oz (340 g) or 6 hot dogs,
preferably sugar free*

Wooden skewers

*I like Applegate brand or beef franks
from US Wellness Meats.

In a fryer or wide heavy-bottomed pan, heat the oil to 375°F (190°C).

Soak the cashews in a bowl with warm water for 20 minutes. Drain completely of any
excess water, patting the cashews dry with paper towels.

Add the cashews, flours, baking powder, salt and eggs to a blender. Blend for about
30 seconds or until completely smooth. Scrape down the sides of the blender and
briefly blend again. Pour the batter into a tall glass.

Use a paper towel to wipe off any excess moisture from the hot dogs so that the
batter sticks to them. Insert the skewers into the hot dogs (depending on the size of
your pan, you can always cut the hot dogs in half, as seen in the pictures).

Working in batches, dip the hot dogs into the batter, swirling around a few times so
that they are evenly coated. Place into the hot oil, completely submerging the hot dog.

Fry for 4 to 6 minutes or until golden brown. Place on a wire rack, allowing any
excess oil to drip off so the hot dogs do not become soggy.

Batter and fry the remaining hot dogs.

Serve warm with Kicking Barbecue Sauce (page 118), mustard or any desired sauce.

CLASSIC PEPPERONI PIZZA

Nut Free

One afternoon while watching football with my husband, I finally got so tired of seeing constant pizza commercials that I ran to the kitchen and started making pizza. Well, this crust took awhile to perfect, but I wanted it to have that chewy crust texture that makes pizza the perfect comfort food. Feel free to play around with your favorite toppings, because the options are endless.

MAKES ONE 10-INCH (25.5-CM) ROUND PIZZA

Yeast Mixture

1 cup (237 ml) warm water

2 tsp (6 g) quick-rise yeast

2 tsp (8 g) coconut sugar

1 tsp (5 g) grass-fed gelatin

Crust Ingredients

¾ cup (102 g) arrowroot flour

⅓ cup (32 g) + 2 tbsp (12 g) coconut flour

2 tsp (6 g) psyllium husk powder

1 tsp (4 g) double-acting baking powder

1 tsp (3 g) xanthan gum*

¼ tsp salt

1 tbsp (15 ml) olive oil

Toppings

½ cup (118 ml) pizza sauce

4 oz (113 g) mozzarella cheese, grated

2 oz (57 g) pepperoni

½ tsp dried Italian herbs

Preheat the oven to 175°F (79°C). Line a baking sheet with parchment paper and set aside.

Make the yeast mixture by whisking together the warm water, yeast, coconut sugar and gelatin. Set it aside for 10 minutes.

In a mixing bowl, sift together all the dry ingredients. After 10 minutes the yeast should have bubbled and doubled in size, this is how you will know if your yeast mixture is good. Add in the yeast mixture and olive oil, using a spatula to stir until a ball of dough starts to form in the center of the bowl.

Cover the dough with a thin towel and turn off the oven (don't forget!). Place the covered dough into the oven to proof (rise), leaving the door slightly cracked for 1 minute, then closing and allowing the dough to proof for 1 hour.

After an hour, remove the dough and heat the oven to 400°F (204°C). Lightly grease your hands with olive oil. Take the ball of dough and place it on the prepared baking sheet, using your hands and fingers to spread it into a 10 inch (25.4 cm) round pizza crust. If the dough is super-sticky, you may need to lightly re-grease your hands with olive oil.

Bake the crust for 14 to 15 minutes or until the edges start to crisp. Now layer on your toppings, starting with the sauce, then cheese and pepperoni.

Bake for 12 to 15 minutes or until the cheese is golden brown and bubbly. Garnish with a sprinkle of Italian herbs.

Allow the pizza to cool for 5 minutes before slicing.

This & That

*Xanthan gum is not an ingredient I typically use, however I wanted to re-create a chewy pizza crust as close to the original as possible. It helps form a perfect pizza crust that you can even pick up with your hands, which is why I chose to leave it as an ingredient. If you are dealing with digestive issues, I do not recommend consuming xanthan gum.

If you want to double this recipe, which I recommend since it goes quickly, make sure to make the dough in two separate bowls.

CREAMY ALFREDO
WITH PROSCIUTTO-WRAPPED CHICKEN

Dairy Free, No Added Sugar

When I was growing up, my mom used to make this comforting, cheesy chicken pasta primavera
that was always my favorite dinner. (Yes, I am a pasta girl at heart!) Although I absolutely love cheese,
I wanted to create a white sauce pasta dish for those who cannot handle dairy. This way of preparing chicken
is one of my favorites when I need a quick dinner, so if you don't have time to make the sauce,
the chicken alone is simply fabulous!

SERVES 3-4

1 (3 lb [1361 g]) spaghetti squash

1 cup (145 g) raw cashew pieces

4 tbsp (58 g) butter, ghee or bacon
grease, divided

¼ cup (34 g) sweet white onion, minced

3 large cloves garlic, crushed

½ cup (118 ml) chicken broth

½ cup (118 ml) full-fat, unsweetened
coconut milk

½ tsp nutritional yeast

¼ rounded tsp salt

⅛ tsp fresh cracked black pepper

1 lb (454 g) chicken breast meat

5 slices prosciutto

Fresh basil to garnish, optional

Preheat the oven to 375°F (190°C) and place the spaghetti squash on a baking sheet. Use the tip of a sharp knife to make a few slits in the squash, allowing heat to escape. Bake for 40 minutes. Cut the ends off the squash and slice in half. Remove the inner seeds and strings and discard. Use a fork to shred the squash into spaghetti-like noodles.

While the squash is baking, soak the cashews in hot water for 30 minutes. Warm a skillet to medium-low heat. Melt 3 tablespoons (45 g) of butter or your grease of choice in the skillet and add the onion and garlic. Sauté for 10 minutes or until the onions are soft and fragrant.

Strain the nuts completely of all water and place in a blender. Add the sautéed butter, onions and garlic to the blender along with the chicken broth, coconut milk, nutritional yeast, salt and pepper. Blend until completely smooth. Scrape down the sides of the blender and briefly blend again.

Add the shredded spaghetti squash to a pan and mix together with desired amount of Alfredo sauce (keeping in mind you may have extra sauce). Warm over low heat until steaming hot and ready to serve.

Turn the skillet up to medium heat and add the remaining tablespoon of butter. Slice the chicken into small strips about 3 by 1 inch (7.6 by 1.2 cm) thick. Slice the prosciutto in half lengthwise and tightly wrap around each chicken strip. Sear the chicken in the skillet for 8 minutes, rotating sides every 2 minutes (depending on the size and thickness of your chicken, you may need to adjust the cooking time).

Serve chicken over the hot spaghetti squash noodles and garnish with fresh basil, if desired.

This & That

This dish is also great served over zucchini noodles or other spiralized vegetable.

Cappello's makes a fabulous grain- and gluten-free fettuccine that is the perfect noodle choice for Alfredo sauce.

CHOCOLATE NUTTER BUTTER CUPS

Nut Free, Dairy Free

A classic favorite—these chocolate nutter butter candies made with real ingredients are a dream too good to be true! Pure chocolate is made from cacao butter, which is rich in omega fatty acids, antioxidants and minerals. Cacao is a superfood that boosts your immune system and mood, bringing happiness to your day. So go ahead and enjoy these sweet bites of chocolate confection—making sure to share a few too!

MAKES 12 MINI CANDY CUPS

½ cup (59 g) raw cacao butter, chopped

5 tbsp (25 g) raw cacao powder

2 tbsp (30 ml) raw honey

1 tsp (5 ml) vanilla extract

½ cup (90 g) creamy nut butter of choice (use Sunflower seed butter for nut free)

Fleur de sel (or coarse sea salt), to sprinkle on top

Place mini muffin liners in a mini muffin pan. If you don't have a mini muffin pan, you can also place them on a baking sheet—just be careful as you fill them up later.

Heat a small amount of water in a small saucepan until it begins to lightly simmer. Add the raw cacao butter to a heat-proof bowl and place the bowl over the simmering water. Once the cacao butter is melted, remove the bowl from the heat and stir in the cacao powder, raw honey and vanilla extract until completely smooth. Set the chocolate aside to cool for 10 minutes.

Using a small spoon, drizzle a small amount of chocolate into the bottom of the muffin liner, filling it slightly less than half full. Set aside the remaining half of the chocolate. Place the muffin tin in the freezer in a flat location to harden for 10 minutes.

Remove the cups from the freezer and add a small spoonful of your nut butter of choice each cup. Drizzle with the remaining chocolate and sprinkle with sea salt if desired. Place in the freezer for 5 more minutes.

THIN-CRUST BBQ PIZZA WITH CRISPY BACON

Dairy Free

You may be looking at the ingredient list, thinking, sauerkraut in pizza? Well, almond flour pizza
is always a little heavy to me, so my dad suggested I add sauerkraut to the dough, which sounded crazy!
But I tried it and it actually helps the dough to stay together quite nicely. I recommend using Bubbies brand
of sauerkraut, which you can find in the refrigerated section of most health food stores,
or another sauerkraut that is slightly crunchy.

MAKES ONE 10 INCH (25.5 CM) ROUND PIZZA

Thin-Crust Pizza

½ (heaping full) cup (68 g) plain
sauerkraut, strained completely of
all juices

1½ cups (165 g) almond flour

¼ cup (34 g) arrowroot flour

½ tsp celtic sea salt

1 tsp (3 g) garlic powder

1 egg

1 tbsp (15 ml) olive oil + more for
greasing hands

Toppings

¼ cup (59 ml) Kicking Barbecue Sauce
(page 118)

½ cup (68 g) leftover Pulled Pork
(page 102)

1 small shallot, thinly sliced

3 oz (85 g) mozzarella, shredded*

6 slices bacon, cooked and crumbled

Cilantro, to garnish

*Omit for dairy free

Preheat the oven to 350°F (176°C). Line a baking sheet with parchment paper.

Add the sauerkraut to a nut milk bag or fine mesh cloth. Strain out the excess juice, and
keep straining, making sure that all juice is removed. Now measure out ½ heaping full
cup (68 g).

Add the strained sauerkraut, flours, salt, garlic, egg and olive oil to the bowl of a
food processor. Pulse several times, then scrape down the sides and bottom of the
bowl. Pulse again until a ball of dough starts to form, being careful not to overmix,
because the flours will turn gummy. Use a spatula to scrape the dough out of the
processor, forming it into a ball.

Rub your hands with a bit of olive oil, then take the dough into your hands, coating
the outside with the olive oil from your hands.

Flatten the dough onto the prepared baking sheet using the tips of your fingers to
gently and patiently spread into a thin circular crust, 10 inches (25.5 cm) in diameter.
If necessary, lightly re-oil your hands.

Bake the crust for 15 to 17 minutes, or until the edges start to crisp, then remove
from the oven.

Turn the oven heat up to 375°F (190°C). Layer your toppings onto the pizza crust,
starting with the barbecue sauce, pulled pork, shallots, mozzarella and, finally,
the bacon. Bake for 15 minutes or until golden brown and bubbly.

Cool for 5 minutes before slicing. Garnish with fresh cilantro, if desired.

This & That

If you decide to use Italian-flavored toppings, I recommend adding some
dried Italian herbs and oregano to the dough.

This pizza can easily be made dairy free by omitting the cheese. Just watch
the toppings carefully so they do not burn.

ROASTED STRAWBERRY SNICKERDOODLE ICE CREAM SANDWICHES

Dairy Free

Sugar, spice and everything oh-so-nice—luscious strawberry ice cream is sandwiched between layers of maple snickerdoodle cookies for a sweet delight with each bite! These cookies are quite simple to make, so gather around and feel free to let the little ones in your life help you bake away.

MAKES 6 ICE CREAM SANDWICHES

Roasted Strawberry Ice Cream

1 recipe Vanilla Ice Cream (page 144)

1 lb (454 g) fresh strawberries, stems removed

1 tbsp (13 g) maple sugar

Snickerdoodle Cookies

4 tbsp (58 g) butter, or palm shortening for dairy free

¼ cup (50 g) maple sugar

1 cup (110 g) almond flour

⅓ cup (45 g) arrowroot flour

1½ tbsp (9 g) coconut flour

¼ tsp baking soda

¼ tsp baking powder

Pinch of salt

1 egg

2 tsp (8 g) maple sugar + ½ tsp ground cinnamon, for dusting

Prepare the ice cream batter according to the instructions on page 144. While it is cooling, preheat the oven to 375°F (190°C). Slice the strawberries into quarters, or eighths, depending on their size. Place the strawberries on a baking sheet and sprinkle with maple sugar. Roast for 30 minutes, stirring halfway through. Use a fork to smash the strawberries, releasing more of their juices. Cool completely.

To make the cookies, turn down the oven heat to 350°F (176°C), adjust the rack to the middle position and line a baking sheet with parchment paper. Slice the butter into small cubes and set it aside to soften for 20 minutes. Sprinkle the maple sugar on top.

In a separate bowl, sift together all dry ingredients. Use a hand mixer to cream the butter and sugar. Add in the flour and egg and briefly blend again until a smooth cookie batter has formed.

Using a 1½ tablespoon (20 g) cookie scoop, scoop the cookie batter and drop it onto the parchment-lined baking sheet. Flatten the cookies gently with your fingertips and generously sprinkle each cookie with the maple sugar and cinnamon mixture.

Bake the cookies for 10 to 12 minutes. Then place them on a cooling rack to cool completely.

Finish preparing the ice cream by adding the vanilla batter to the ice cream maker. Churn the ice cream until it begins to thicken, then add the strawberries and all the roasting juices to the ice cream maker to finish churning. Place the ice cream in the freezer for 20 to 30 minutes to firm up.

Add a scoop of ice cream between two cookies and place in the freezer for 10 minutes before enjoying. Store any extra ice cream in the freezer.

This & That

The roasted strawberries themselves are delicious served with fluffy whipped cream and garnished with chocolate shavings for a quick, colorful and gourmet dessert option.

TOMATO BASIL SOUP

Nut Free, Dairy Free, No Added Sugar

Warm and comforting, this soup is my favorite, especially on a chilly day. I like to make
grilled cheese out of the Crispy Bacon Sweet Potato Waffles (page 130) to dip in the warm soup,
or top with Crackling Pork Belly Croutons (page 86) for a dairy-free option.

SERVES 6-8

2 lbs (907 g) fresh, ripe tomatoes

1 small sweet white onion

1 large carrot

5 large cloves garlic, peeled

¼ cup (59 ml) olive oil

1½ tsp (8 g) salt, divided

2 (15 oz [425 g]) cans tomato puree

1½ cup (355 ml) full-fat, unsweetened
coconut milk

½ cup (68 g) fresh basil, plus more
for garnish

½ tsp dried oregano

¼ tsp black pepper

1 cup (136 g) Crackling Pork Belly
Croutons (page 86), for serving

Preheat the oven to 400°F (204°C). Slice the tomatoes in half, discarding the stems.
Cube the onion and carrot. Add the tomatoes, onion, carrot and garlic cloves to a
large roasting pan. Toss together with olive oil and half of the salt. Roast for
40 minutes, stirring halfway through.

Cool the vegetables for 10 minutes before transferring to a large pot. Add in
the remaining ingredients. Use an immersion blender to puree until the soup is
completely smooth. If you do not have an immersion blender, you can use a blender,
but make sure your tomatoes are cool and you work in batches to avoid a mess!
Simmer on low for 30 minutes before serving.

Top your bowl of soup with a garnish of fresh basil and Crackling Pork Belly Croutons.

GARLIC BREAD BITES

Nut Free, No Added Sugar

During my freshman year of college, I think I practically survived on the cafeteria's actually quite delicious cheesy bread dipped in ranch dressing. Now, I don't even want to think about what ingredients were actually in those foods, so I decided to re-create it! This cheesy bread is a great way to get your kids involved in the cooking process or to introduce others to healthy eating. Plus, there are hidden vegetables involved, so what's not to love?

MAKES 10 SMALL BREAD BITES

4 cups (544 g) riced cauliflower, heaping full

4 oz (113 g) Parmesan cheese, shredded

4 large cloves garlic, crushed

2 tbsp (17 g) arrowroot flour

1 tbsp (9 g) coconut flour

2 tsp (6 g) psyllium husk powder

1 tsp (3 g) Italian herbs

½ tsp oregano

½ tsp salt

½ tsp baking powder

1 egg, whisked

Ranch Dressing (page 168) or pizza sauce, for serving and dipping

Preheat the oven to 375°F (190°C) and line a baking sheet with parchment paper.

In a steamer pot, bring a few inches of water to a boil to use for steaming the cauliflower. Use the grating attachment of a food processor to rice the cauliflower and then measure out 4 cups (544 g), saving any extra cauliflower for later use.

Add the riced cauliflower to a steamer basket, placing it over the boiling water, but not actually touching the water. Place a lid on top and steam for 6 minutes. Remove the steamer basket and lid from the boiling water and set it aside to cool for 15 minutes.

Meanwhile, in a large mixing bowl, mix together the shredded Parmesan, garlic, flours, psyllium, herbs, salt and baking powder.

Place the steamed cauliflower in a nut milk bag or in a fine mesh cloth and squeeze out any liquid. Continue squeezing for a while, then when you think all the excess water is finally out, squeeze a few more times. Once the water is completely removed, you will be left with about a cup of cauliflower.

Add the cauliflower and whisked egg to the bowl and mix, forming a small ball of dough.

Use your hands to shape and firmly pack the cauliflower dough into small bread bites about 2 inches (5 cm) long.

Bake for 28 to 30 minutes or until the tops are very golden brown.

Allow the bread bites to cool for 5 minutes before serving. Dip into Ranch Dressing or warmed pizza sauce.

CRISPY CHEESE CRACKERS

No Added Sugar

Snacks are something I miss the most, and these grain-free cheese crackers truly taste like
their gluten-filled, packaged friends. They are even slightly yellow with the addition of smoked paprika.
Macadamia nuts are low in phytic acid, an anti-nutrient, making these nuts a great snack and very easy
to digest. These tasty crackers are rich in fats and proteins to keep you satisfied, but be warned—you
may be reaching for more than a few handfuls!

MAKES ABOUT 40 CRACKERS

---

1 cup (145 g) raw macadamia nuts

4 oz (113 g) sharp cheddar cheese,
shredded

2 tbsp (17 g) arrowroot flour

1 tbsp (6 g) coconut flour

½ tsp grass-fed gelatin

¼ tsp salt

¼ tsp smoked paprika

Preheat the oven to 275°F (135°C) and line a baking sheet with parchment paper.
Adjust the oven rack to the middle position.

Add the macadamia nuts to the bowl of a food processor and blend for about 30
seconds or until the nuts become a smooth, flour-like mixture. Add the remaining
ingredients and blend for an additional 30 seconds or until a ball of dough begins
to form in the food processor.

Remove the dough and use your hands to shape into a circle. Place on the parchment
paper and use your hands to flatten into a very thin, rectangular shape, about
9 by 12 inches (22.8 by 30.5 cm). Be patient because this process takes some time.

Using the tip only of a sharp knife, gently slice the dough into about 1½ inch
(3.8 cm) squares.

Bake for 48 to 52 minutes, depending on how thin you were able to make your
dough, or until the edges start to brown. Remove from the oven and set aside to cool
completely, allowing the crackers to firm up and become crispy.

The squares you made prior to baking will mostly be gone now, but use the lines as
a guide to break them into crackers. Once completely cooled, break the crackers into
pieces and store any extras in an airtight container.

This & That
Be sure to use an aged sharp cheddar cheese; regular cheddar will add
a bit too much moisture to the crackers.

SWEET AND SALTY COCONUT SNACK MIX

Nut Free, Dairy Free, No Added Sugar

Watching movies just isn't the same without a bowl of crunchy snack mix—which usually is filled with wheat,
corn, sugar and preservatives. So I came up with toasted coconut flakes as the base for this snack mix.
It stores well in an airtight container and is great to make a big bowl of before movie night,
to send with your kids to school or even to use as an ice cream topping!

MAKES ABOUT 3½ CUPS (590 G)

2 heaping full cups (110 g) thick,
unsweetened coconut flakes

1 cup (136 g) slivered almonds*
(omit for nut free)

1½ tsp (8 g) sea salt

1 oz (453 g) freeze-dried strawberries

½ cup (68 g) finely chopped dark
chocolate**

*Omit for nut free and increase the
coconut flakes to 3 cups (165 g)

**I recommend using Pure 7 chocolate
bars.

Warm a large nonstick skillet to medium-low heat for a good 5 minutes, ensuring that
the pan is evenly heated. Toss the coconut, almonds and salt together.

Add the coconut mix to the pan, probably working in batches so that the flakes and
almonds are all touching the pan's heat. Toast for 5 to 7 minutes, stirring occasionally
so that it does not burn, or until golden brown.

Place the toasted coconut into a bowl and cool completely. Add the freeze-dried
strawberries and chocolate and toss together.

This & That

The salt usually settles to the bottom after some time, so if you are storing
this, just give it a quick stir before eating.

The Thankful Table

Autumn Creations for Fall Feasts

Preparing for Thanksgiving can be a fun yet stressful time, especially when dietary restrictions are involved. With a little planning and preparation the day or two before Thanksgiving, these recipes are actually quite simple, full of flavor and offer a broad variety so that everyone can enjoy. I personally think these fall re-creations are much tastier than their grain-filled versions.

I am daily reminded of how thankful I am for my health and the many blessings of life. My hope is that these fall recipes bring some healthy creations to your Thanksgiving table, as you eat, laugh and always remember to give thanks.

APPLE PIE

Thanksgiving would not be complete without apple pie! Yes, just like any gluten-free baked good, this dough is a bit more difficult to work with, but with a little patience, you will once again have apple pie on your table. Garnish with a scoop of Vanilla Ice Cream (page 144) or a drizzle of Salted Caramel Sauce (page 144), making it à la mode.

MAKES ONE 9-INCH (22.8-CM) PIE

Crust
8 tbsp (115 g) butter

¼ cup (50 g) maple sugar

2 eggs

2 tsp (10 ml) vanilla extract

2 cups (220 g) blanched almond flour

1 cup (136 g) + 2 tbsp (17 g) arrowroot flour

⅓ cup (38 g) chestnut flour

2 tbsp (12 g) coconut flour

¼ tsp ground cinnamon

¼ tsp salt

Filling
2½ lbs (1134 g) Granny Smith apples (about 5 apples)

2 tbsp (25 g) maple sugar

1 tbsp (9 g) arrowroot flour

1 tbsp (15 ml) lemon juice

2 tsp (5 g) ground cinnamon

1 tsp (5 ml) vanilla extract

¼ tsp ground nutmeg

1 egg, whisked, for brushing on crust

This & That
Chestnut flour can dry out quickly if it is overcooked, so I recommend watching the pie carefully at the end, keeping in mind your individual oven specifics.

To make the crust, slice the butter into very small cubes. Add the butter, maple sugar, eggs and vanilla extract to a bowl and set aside to come to room temperature for 40 minutes. In a separate bowl, sift together all the dry ingredients for the crust.

Use a hand mixer to cream the butter, sugar and eggs together. Add in the dry ingredients and briefly mix, then scrape down the sides and bottom of the bowl. Continue mixing until the dough goes from crumbly to a round ball, being careful not to overwork the dough.

Divide the dough in half, shaping into two round cylinder shapes. Tightly wrap in plastic wrap and refrigerate for 45 minutes.

Next, peel and core the apples for the filling. Slice them into very thin slices, about ⅛- to ¼-inch (3- to 6-mm) thick, or as thin as you possibly can make them. Add the apples to a large mixing bowl, stirring in the remaining filling ingredients. Set the apples aside to marinate while the dough is chilling.

Preheat the oven to 350°F (176°C), arranging the oven rack to the middle position.

Take one of the wrapped dough rounds from the refrigerator and roll out between two layers of parchment paper until slightly larger than your 9-inch (22.8-cm) pie dish. Chill in the refrigerator for 5 minutes. Remove the top layer of parchment paper and gently place the pie dish on top of the dough. Grab the edges of the parchment paper and carefully invert the pie dish. Before removing the parchment paper, press the dough into the bottom of the dish and up the sides, then remove the paper. Pile the apple filling on top.

Remove the second round of dough and repeat the process of rolling out the dough between two layers of parchment paper and chilling in the refrigerator for 5 minutes. Remove the top layer of parchment paper. Using both hands, take the dough and carefully invert it on top of the apple filling, then remove the paper. Use your fingers to pinch together the edges of the pie as well as any small tears. Using the tip of a sharp knife, make 6 cuts in the piecrust to allow air to escape.

Place the pie dish on a baking sheet, tent the pie with a piece of foil and bake for 30 minutes. Remove the foil and brush the crust with the whisked egg, keeping in mind you will not use all the egg wash. Continue baking for an additional 30 minutes or until the crust is golden brown.

Cool the pie for 20 to 30 minutes before slicing and serving.

CIDER MILL DONUT HOLES

Nut Free, Dairy Free

When I moved away to Michigan for college, I discovered fall, and with that came jumping
through endless piles of crunchy leaves, weekend trips to the cider mill and of course, these fantastic
fried donuts covered in cinnamon sugar sprinkles. I made them into donut holes so that
if you don't have a donut pan, you can still easily make them!

MAKES 14-16 DONUT HOLES

4 cups (946 ml) coconut oil, for frying

½ cup (50 g) + 3 tbsp (18 g) coconut flour

¼ cup (34 g) arrowroot flour

¼ cup (50 g) maple sugar

1 tsp (3 g) ground cinnamon

½ tsp baking soda

Pinch of salt

4 eggs

½ cup (118 ml) apple cider

2 tbsp (30 ml) raw honey

1 tsp (5 ml) vanilla extract

Sprinkles
3 tbsp (38 g) maple sugar

1 tbsp (8 g) ground cinnamon

Warm a heavy-bottomed pan or fryer with the coconut oil, making sure you have about 3 inches (7.6 cm) worth of oil. Slowly heat the oil until the temperature reaches 375°F (190°C).

In a mixing bowl, sift together the flours, maple sugar, cinnamon, baking soda and salt. In a separate bowl, blend together the eggs, apple cider, raw honey and vanilla extract until smooth. Add the flour to the egg batter and blend until a smooth batter forms. Scrape down the sides and bottom of the bowl and let the batter set for 1 minute to allow the flours to soak up the liquids. Briefly blend the batter one last time.

Using a 1½ tablespoon (20 g) cookie scoop, scoop the batter and carefully drop it into the hot oil. Add a few more donut holes to the pan, but don't overcrowd the pan. Keeping your oil temperature stable, fry the donuts for about 4 minutes, flipping after 2 minutes to make sure that all sides are evenly cooked. Remove the donuts with a slotted spoon and place on a paper towel. While the donuts are still warm, sprinkle with the maple cinnamon sugar.

Fry the remaining donuts, sprinkling them with cinnamon sugar once they are done. After all the donuts are cooked and cool enough to touch, roll the donuts in the remaining cinnamon sugar so that all sides are dusted.

Best eaten fresh and warm!

SMOKED TURKEY

Nut Free, Dairy Free

Yes, turkey is the main event on the Thanksgiving table. It's also something that was often very dry to me, until this smoked turkey came along! Although the process does take a bit of preparation, it actually frees up a lot of space in your kitchen to work on other dishes and desserts. When I tested this recipe with friends and family, everyone decided it did not need a gravy. This really allows the smoky flavor to shine through. When smoked correctly, this turkey is the most moist and delicious I have ever had, and I must say leftovers might even be better!

SERVES 10-12

Turkey Brine

1 gallon (4 L) water

1 cup (241 g) kosher salt

1 cup (237 ml) unsweetend apple juice

1 cup (237 ml) maple syrup

1 tbsp (9 g) black pepper

Plenty of ice

Smoked Turkey

1 (12 lb [5 kg]) turkey

1 small sweet white onion, cubed

1 small green apple, cored and cubed

2 tbsp (30 ml) maple syrup

3 tbsp (45 g) salt

1 tbsp (9 g) black pepper

1 tsp (3 g) paprika

1 cup (236 ml) unsweetend apple juice, for injecting and smoking turkey

This & That

The flavor of this turkey is so amazing that it really does not need any gravy. Allow the smoky flavor of the meat to be the main event.

Hickory wood is our wood of choice when it comes to smoking a turkey, but you can also use pecan wood.

The day before you are going to smoke your turkey, make sure your turkey is completely thawed before brining. Remove the gizzards and any innards of the turkey and discard.

In a large stockpot, heat one quart (946 ml) of the water, stirring in the salt until it dissolves. Add the apple juice, maple syrup and pepper. Remove from the heat, adding in the remaining water and ice until the water is chilled. Place the turkey in the brine, adding more water until it is fully submerged. Refrigerate for 24 hours. Depending on the size of your turkey, you can also place the turkey and brine in a large plastic bag in a cooler, covering the top with ice.

The day of smoking, remove the turkey from the brine, draining any excess water and patting completely dry with paper towels.

While the turkey dries, prepare your smoker with hickory wood, bringing it to a stable temperature of 225°F (107°C).

Stuff the turkey with the onion and apple cubes; depending on the size of your turkey, you may not use them all.

Next, rub the turkey with the maple syrup. Stir together the salt, pepper and paprika and sprinkle over all sides of the turkey, seasoning every possible area.

Place the turkey on the grill grates, maintaining a constant temperature of 225°F (107°C). Be sure to constantly tend to the fire to prevent the temperature from dropping too low. Every 30 minutes, spray the entire turkey with a bit of apple juice. Every 2 hours, inject a bit of apple juice into both sides of the breast meat.

Smoke the turkey until the breast meat is 165°F (73°C) and the legs are 175°F (79°C), but keep in mind that the temperature will continue to rise after the turkey is off the heat, so I usually pull it off a few degrees before. This process can take anywhere from 4 to 7 hours, depending on the size of your turkey, smoking environment and ability to maintain heat, so trust the internal temperature reading, not the cooking time.

Place the turkey on a wire rack to allow it to cool for 15 to 20 minutes before carving, leaving it uncovered so the skin does not become soggy.

Carve the turkey in individual sections—breast, thigh, wings and so forth—and serve.

SAUSAGE, APPLE, MUSHROOM STUFFING

Nut Free, Dairy Free, No Added Sugar

I never really liked stuffing until I created this recipe, which forever changed my mind, and now I pretty much want to eat it all the time. Made with grain-free bread, savory sausage and lots of fresh herbs, this stuffing won't leave you stuffed at all! Although the ingredient list may seem daunting, it is truly worth all the preparation, and leftovers make for the best breakfast hash topped with a fried egg.

SERVES 8-10

½ cup (118 ml) chicken broth

¼ cup (59 ml) cognac*

3 eggs

1 loaf Nut-Free Sandwich Bread (page 30)

1 lb (454 g) mild Italian pork sausage

4 tbsp (58 g) butter or ghee**

1 sweet white onion, minced

2 cloves garlic, crushed

2 tbsp (17 g) fresh sage, finely chopped

1 tsp (3 g) fresh rosemary, finely chopped

½ tsp fresh thyme, finely chopped

1 tsp (5 g) salt

8 cremini mushrooms, minced

2 green apples, pealed, cored and cut into small cubes

Cognac gives this dish a rich gourmet flavor, but you can also substitute a dry white wine. If you are opposed to cooking with alcohol, you may substitute extra chicken broth.

**For strict dairy free, I recommend using duck fat or bacon grease.*

Preheat the oven to 350°F (176°C) and warm a large skillet to medium heat. Line a baking sheet with parchment paper. Whisk together the chicken broth, cognac and eggs and set aside.

Slice the bread into very small cubes, about 1 inch (2.5 cm) thick. Arrange the bread cubes evenly throughout the baking sheet and toast them in the oven for 10 minutes.

Add the sausage to the skillet, crumbling into small pieces. Cook the sausage completely, then use a slotted spoon to remove it from the pan, placing the sausage crumbles into a large mixing bowl and discarding any grease.

Next, brown the butter in the skillet, swirling the butter around the pan until it starts to bubble. Continue cooking the butter until it is a rich golden brown color and gives off a nutty aroma.

Add in the onion, garlic, sage, rosemary, thyme and salt. Sauté for 5 minutes or until the onions begin to soften. Add the mushrooms and apples and continue sautéing for 10 additional minutes.

Transfer the sauté mixture to the mixing bowl with the sausage and stir to mix. Add in the toasted bread cubes. Drizzle in the egg batter and lightly stir to evenly coat the stuffing mixture.

Place all ingredients in a 9 by 13 inch (22.8 by 33 cm) baking dish and cover with foil.

Bake for 30 minutes, then remove the foil and bake for an additional 10 minutes.

Serve warm.

This & That

Prepare your bread two days ahead of time to save time on preparation and washing dishes.

This is one of those dishes that you can wrap with foil to keep warm while you are waiting for the rest of your dishes to finish cooking. If you need to reheat it, I recommend spraying the top with a bit of water or chicken broth to prevent the bread from drying out.

PUMPKIN MOUSSE CHEESECAKE

A blend between pumpkin pie and cheesecake, this version is quite light and sweetened ever so beautifully.
If you make the cheesecake ahead of time, I highly recommend tucking it away—otherwise you might find a
slice or two has disappeared! This cheesecake is one of the most requested desserts when friends come over,
and it will have you dreaming of a slice for breakfast.

MAKES A 9-INCH (22.8-CM) CHEESECAKE

Cheesecake Crust

4 tbsp (60 g) butter

1 cup (136 g) raw pecans

½ cup (68 g) raw almonds

½ cup (68 g) raw hazelnuts

8 pitted Medjool dates (about
½ cup [68 g])

2 tbsp (30 ml) coconut oil

2 tsp (5 g) ground cinnamon

½ tsp ground nutmeg

1 tsp (5 ml) vanilla

Pumpkin Filling

8 oz (226 g) mascarpone

8 oz (226 g) full-fat cream cheese

¼ cup (59 ml) + 2 tbsp (30 ml) maple
syrup

1 tsp (5 g) grass-fed gelatin

8 oz (228 ml) grass-fed heavy whipping
cream

½ cup (68 g) full-fat sour cream

¾ cup (102 g) pumpkin puree

1 tbsp (15 ml) vanilla extract

1½ tsp (4 g) ground cinnamon

¼ tsp ground nutmeg

⅛ tsp ground cardamom

Additional whipped cream to garnish,
optional

Preheat the oven to 350°F (176°C).

Remove the mascarpone and cream cheese for the filling from the refrigerator and
place on the counter to soften for 1½ hours. Cut the butter for the crust into small
slices and set aside to soften for 10 minutes.

Place all crust ingredients into the bowl of a food processor. Pulse several times, then
scrape down the sides and bottom of the bowl. Blend again for about 30 seconds or
until the nuts go from crumbly to smooth but not a nut butter–like consistency. Your
crust is ready when it starts to move around like a ball in the food processor.

Transfer the crust to a 9 inch (22.8 cm), nonstick springform pan. Use your fingertips
to press the crust out evenly in the bottom of the pan.

Bake on the middle rack for 16 to 17 minutes or just until the edges of the crust start
to brown. Cool the crust for 1 hour.

After your cheeses have come to room temperature, start making the filling. Add the
maple syrup to a small saucepan, sprinkling the gelatin on top, and set aside for
a few minutes to allow it to bloom. Heat the syrup over low heat and stir until the
gelatin is dissolved.

Pour the heavy whipping cream into a bowl and whip until stiff peaks begin to form.
In a seperate bowl, add the mascarpone, cream cheese, sour cream, pumpkin, maple
syrup and gelatin, vanilla, cinnamon, nutmeg and cardamom. Use a hand mixer to
blend until smooth. Scrape down the sides and bottom of the bowl and blend again
on high for 30 seconds so that the filling is thick and creamy. Fold in the whipped
cream until smooth.

Pour the pumpkin filling on top of the cooled crust, gently smoothing out the top.
Cover with plastic wrap and refrigerate for a minimum of 4 hours.

When you are ready to serve, run a knife along the edges of the pan, then remove
the springform pan's outer circle, slice and serve.

This & That

For those of you sensitive to dairy, I sincerely apologize, but I cheesecake is
so often filled with sugar that I wanted to include a healthier version of the
classic dessert!

ROASTED BEET SALAD WITH PEARS AND CANDIED PECANS

Dairy Free

The pecans have a bit of spice and not too much sweetness, which adds the perfect crunch to this salad.
The best part is that you can prepare most of the ingredients ahead of time and just toss and serve.
I love to turn this salad into a meal by adding grilled chicken or leftover smoked turkey (page 204)!

SERVES 6

Candied Pecans

1 cup (136 g) pecan halves

1 tbsp (15 ml) maple syrup

1 tbsp (13 g) maple sugar

½ tsp salt

¼ tsp ground cinnamon

Dash of ground nutmeg

Roasted Beets

2 small beets

2 tsp (10 ml) olive oil

¼ tsp salt

Salad

5 oz (142 g) fresh mixed greens

1 pear, cored and cubed

2 tbsp (17 g) fresh basil, thinly sliced

4 oz (113 g) feta cheese, crumbled
(omit for dairy free)

½ cup (118 ml) Balsamic Basil
Vinaigrette (page 74)

Preheat the oven to 300°F (148°C) and line two baking sheets with parchment paper. Mix together all ingredients for the candied pecans, evenly coating the nuts. Spread them throughout one of the prepared baking sheets so that none of the nuts are piled on top of each other.

Bake for 40 minutes, stirring halfway through. Set the nuts aside to cool.

Once the nuts are done, turn up the oven to 375°F (190°C). Scrub and rinse the beets, cutting off the ends. Slice the beets as thin as possible and place on the baking sheet. Brush both sides with olive oil and sprinkle with salt. Roast for 40 minutes, rotating the beets halfway through.

Assemble the salad by adding the mixed greens to a large bowl, then layering on the roasted beets, cubed pears, candied pecans, basil and feta crumbles. Toss with dressing and serve.

This & That

The candied pecans can be prepared a few days in advance. I usually double or triple the recipe to have extras on hand or to give away as tasty gifts!

SWEET POTATOES AU GRATIN

Nut Free, No Added Sugar

Many Thanksgiving sweet potato recipes are sweet, but I prefer a savory style. This side dish
is decadent with rich layers of creamy goodness, finished with a slightly crispy crust, and perfectly pairs
with the smoked turkey. Do not limit this dish just to your Thanksgiving feast; it is great to prepare
for any party or weeknight comfort food.

SERVES 8-12

3 lbs (1361 g) or about 3 large sweet potatoes

6 tbsp (86 g) butter, melted

½ cup (68 g) full-fat sour cream

2 large cloves garlic, crushed

1 tsp (5 g) salt

½ tsp paprika

12 oz (340 g) sharp cheddar cheese, shredded

Preheat the oven to 400°F (204°C).

Thinly slice the sweet potatoes into ¼ inch (6 mm) rounds, or as thin as you can possibly make them. Stir together the melted butter, sour cream, garlic, salt and paprika.

In a 9 by 13 inch (20.8 by 33 cm) pan, start creating the bottom layer by adding a layer of sweet potatoes. Add about ¼ of the butter and sour cream mixture, spreading it out evenly across the sweet potatoes. Then sprinkle on ¼ of the shredded cheese. Repeat this process until you have created 4 layers. Cover the dish with foil.

Bake for 60 minutes, then remove the foil and continue baking for an additional 10 minutes or until the sweet potatoes are tender to touch with a fork and the cheese is bubbly and golden brown.

This & That

This dish can be prepared a day ahead and left uncooked in the refrigerator. Simply bring the dish to room temperature before placing it in the oven.

CRISPY BRUSSELS SPROUTS WITH PANCETTA AND BALSAMIC GLAZE

Nut Free, Dairy Free, No Added Sugar

For the longest time, I had the biggest fear of Brussels sprouts, until eating them at this dreamy little French restaurant in San Diego. But these crispy Brussels sprouts take the vegetable to a whole new level—with salty pancetta with a rich balsamic glaze for the perfect sweet and savory combination. This is such a simple dish to toss together at the last minute while you are waiting for your bird to finish!

SERVES 6

1½ lb (681 g) Brussels sprouts

4 oz (114 g) thick-cut pancetta

1 tbsp (15 ml) olive oil

1 tsp (5 g) sea salt

Fresh cracked black pepper, to taste

2 tbsp (30 ml) balsamic glaze or reduction

Preheat the oven to 400°F (204°C). Cut the stems off the Brussels sprouts and slice into halves, thirds or quarters, depending on their size. Keep the leaves that may fall off—those turn delightfully crispy as they roast. Slice the pancetta into small cubes.

On a large rimmed baking sheet or roasting pan, toss together the sprouts, pancetta, olive oil, salt and pepper. Spread out evenly with none of the sprouts piled on top of each other.

Roast for 25 minutes or until they start to turn crispy.

Drizzle with balsamic glaze.

PUMPKIN SPICE LATTES

Nut Free, Dairy Free

Something about life turns magical with the changing of seasons—
enjoying cold mornings gathered around hot cups of coffee and watching the falling brightly colored leaves.
It is that time of year when many people go crazy for a pumpkin latte. Real pumpkin puree, spices and maple
syrup re-create this coffee shop classic without all the added sugars and preservatives. So cozy up with a
movie or a good book and enjoy this fall cup of cheer.

SERVES 4

1 (13.5-oz [399-ml]) can full-fat, unsweetened coconut milk

2-4 tbsp (30-45 ml) maple syrup, depending on desired sweetness

2 tbsp (17 g) pumpkin puree

2 tbsp (29 g) butter or ghee*

1 tsp (5 ml) vanilla extract

½ tsp ground cinnamon

¼ tsp ground nutmeg

2 cups (473 ml) hot, strongly brewed coffee or 4 espresso shots

4 oz (113 g) whipped coconut cream or grass-fed heavy whipping cream, for garnish (optional)

Ground cinnamon, for garnish (optional)

*Use coconut oil for strict dairy free.

Add the coconut milk, maple syrup, pumpkin puree, butter, vanilla extract, cinnamon and nutmeg to a blender. Blend until smooth.

Warm the pumpkin milk over medium-low heat for 10 minutes or until the milk starts to steam.

Meanwhile, prepare your coffee or espresso.

Once your milk is hot, place it back into the blender and blend for about 10 seconds to froth the milk, making sure your hand is on the lid to avoid any messes.

Divide the hot coffee and milk between 4 cups. Garnish with whipped cream and cinnamon, if desired!

This & That

If you do not drink coffee, you can serve this creamer with chai tea or your favorite herbal tea.

A Very Merry Christmas to All

Festive Eats for a Joyful Season

So many memories are made during the holiday season as you gather with friends and family around the table and enjoy good food, tasty baked goods and laughter. With my diabetes diagnosis, the holidays were always a difficult time for me. I thought the foods I once held dear were gone forever. But with a little planning, preparation and creativity, you can once again enjoy many of your festive favorites. I hope these creations bring joy to your holiday table, always remembering the reason for the season!

GINGERBREAD CARAMEL CAKE

Probably the first thought that comes to mind when hearing "gingerbread" is the classic cutout cookie and childhood favorite. This cake is simple to make, and layered with maple caramel and whipped cream rather than a complicated frosting. It's a great addition to your dessert table.

MAKES A 9 INCH (22.8 CM) ROUND DOUBLE-LAYERED CAKE

Coconut oil for greasing the pan

1 cup (100 g) coconut flour

1 cup (100 g) chestnut flour

1 tbsp (11 g) baking powder

1½ tbsp (13 g) ground ginger

1 tsp (3 g) ground cinnamon

1 tsp (3 g) ground cardamom

½ tsp ground nutmeg

½ tsp sea salt

12 eggs

1 cup (236 ml) molasses

1 cup (237 ml) full-fat, unsweetened coconut milk

8 tbsp (115 g) butter or ghee, melted

2 tsp (10 ml) vanilla extract

Maple Caramel Sauce
6 tbsp (86 g) butter or ghee

6 tbsp (90 ml) maple syrup

1½ tsp (7 ml) vanilla extract

12 oz (340 ml) grass-fed heavy whipped cream or whipped coconut cream* for garnish

See explanation on page 132.

Preheat the oven to 350°F (176°C) and arrange the rack to the lower portion of the oven. Brush the bottom and sides of 2 individual 9 inch (22.8 cm) round cake pans with coconut oil.

Sift together all the dry ingredients into a mixing bowl. In a separate large mixing bowl, add the remaining wet ingredients and use a hand mixer to blend until smooth.

Add the flour to the egg batter mixture and blend until a smooth batter forms. Use a spatula to scrape down the bottom and sides of the bowl. Briefly blend again on high speed for about 20 seconds. This traps air, helping the cake to rise and not fall in the center. The batter will be very runny.

Pour half of the batter into one greased cake pan and the remaining half in the other.

Bake for 32 to 36 minutes or until a tester comes out clean, watching carefully. You want the gingerbread to be more on the moist side. Keep in mind that the cake will continue cooking even after it is removed from the oven. Place the cake pans on a cooling rack and cool for 15 minutes before inverting the cakes on the cooling rack to cool completely.

While the cakes are baking, begin making the glaze by melting the butter in a small saucepan over low heat. Stir in the maple syrup.

Gradually turn up the heat to medium-low and continue heating until small bubbles begin to form. Stir the sauce a few times, then allow it to lightly simmer for 5 minutes without touching.

Remove pan from the heat and stir in the vanilla extract. Cool the glaze for 15 to 20 minutes, allowing it to thicken.

While the cakes are still warm, slowly spoon part of the caramel sauce onto each cake, spreading evenly and allowing the cakes to absorb the caramel. Wait 5 minutes before repeating this process two or three times (you may have extra caramel left over).

Carefully transfer the first layered cake to your serving dish. Garnish with half of the whipped cream.

Place the second cake layer on top and garnish with the remaining whipped cream. Slice and enjoy.

This & That

Gingerbread tastes better with time, so allow the flavors to settle in. You can always bake the cake the day before.

Chestnut flour is a sweet, slightly spiced Italian-style flour that brings a unique richness of flavor to this cake. It is made from dried and ground chestnuts and not to be confused with water chestnut flour.

MAPLE SUGAR CHRISTMAS MORNING CINNAMON ROLLS

As a little girl, I used to sit on the counter and help my dad make his famous Christmas morning cinnamon rolls, and this tradition has so many memories for me. It was over Christmas break that I was diagnosed with diabetes and too sick to make cinnamon rolls. I vividly remember shedding a few tears over the thought of never being able to bake them again with my dad. These are a cross between a biscuit and fluffy roll, but with a gooey sweet center. I hope these sweet buns bring joy to you and your loved ones on Christmas morning!

MAKES 10 CINNAMON ROLLS

Cinnamon Roll Dough

4 tbsp (58 g) butter

2 eggs

2 tbsp (25 g) maple sugar

2 cups (220 g) blanched almond flour

¾ cup (102 g) + 2 tbsp (17 g) arrowroot flour

2 tbsp (12 g) coconut flour

1 tsp (3 g) xanthan gum*

¼ tsp baking soda

¼ tsp baking powder

Filling

3 tbsp (43 g) butter

3 tbsp (38 g) maple sugar

2 tsp (5 g) ground cinnamon

Glaze

3 tbsp (43 g) butter

¼ cup (59 ml) maple syrup

1 tsp (5 ml) vanilla extract

1 tsp (3 g) ground cinnamon

This & That

*I typically do not use xanthan gum in recipes, however, this is important to helping the cinnamon rolls stick together. If you have digestive issues, I would not recommend eating these rolls.

Cube the butter into small pieces and add to a bowl along with the eggs and maple sugar. Set aside for 40 minutes. In a separate bowl, sift together the almond, arrowroot and coconut flours, xanthan gum, baking soda and baking powder.

Using a hand mixer, cream the butter and egg mixture until incorporated. Add the butter mixture to the flours and mix until a smooth ball of dough begins to form. Use your hands to shape the dough into a flat, round shape and tightly wrap with plastic wrap. Chill for 30 minutes.

Preheat the oven to 340°F (171°C), adjusting the oven rack to the middle position. Melt the butter for the filling, and in a separate bowl mix the maple sugar and cinnamon.

Roll out the dough between two layers of parchment paper, working very patiently to make a thin, rectangular shape about 11 by 14 inches (28 by 35.5 cm). Transfer the dough and parchment paper to a baking sheet and chill in the refrigerator for 5 minutes. Remove the top layer of parchment paper. Drizzle 2 tablespoons (30 g) of the melted butter onto the dough, using a spatula to evenly spread around. Sprinkle the maple sugar and cinnamon on top.

Very carefully and slowly, use your fingers to roll up the dough, trying to roll it as tight as possible. Use the parchment paper as a guide, lifting up the paper and tightly rolling the dough. Use your fingers to pinch together any minor cracks. Keep in mind that this is not as workable as a gluten dough, but if you are patient, it will work great! Use a sharp knife to cut into 10 cinnamon rolls. Place upright on the parchment-lined baking sheet about 1 inch (2.5 cm) apart from each other. Brush the tops with the remaining butter. Bake for 20 to 22 minutes or just until the tops start to turn golden brown, watching carefully at the end, because you do not want them to overcook and dry out.

While the cinnamon rolls are baking, make the glaze. Melt the butter in a small saucepan. Add the maple syrup, stirring in the same direction until smooth. Bring the syrup to a simmer and lightly simmer for 5 minutes. Remove from the heat and stir in the vanilla and cinnamon until smooth. Set aside to cool while the cinnamon rolls are baking because it will continue to thicken as it cools.

Slowly drizzle a small amount of glaze on the rolls, allowing it to soak in before drizzling more. Brush the sides of the rolls with any remaining glaze.

Allow the cinnamon rolls to cool for 10 minutes before touching or serving them because almond flour is very crumbly when warm. Best served warm and fresh.

CREAMY CHOCOLATE PEPPERMINT TRUFFLES

Nut Free, Dairy Free

A cool peppermint filling is covered in layers of rich chocolate for a healthy twist on the favorite candy.

MAKES 12 TRUFFLES

Creamy Peppermint Filling

¼ cup (46 g) + 2 tbsp (17 g) raw cacao butter, finely chopped

1½ tbsp (22 ml) raw honey

1 cup (220 g) coconut butter

¾ cup (102 g) finely shredded, unsweetened coconut flakes

2 tsp (10 ml) peppermint extract

Chocolate Shell

½ cup (59 g) raw cacao butter, finely chopped

2 tbsp (30 ml) raw honey

¼ cup (24 g) + 1 tbsp (6 g) raw cacao powder

½ tsp peppermint extract

Pinch of salt

First, line a baking sheet with parchment paper and place it in the freezer.

Now, start by making the filling. In a small saucepan, bring about 2 inches (5 cm) of water to a simmer. Add the cacao butter and honey to a heatproof bowl and place over the simmering water. Stir until melted then add the coconut butter, coconut flakes and peppermint extract. Mix until smooth, then refrigerate the filling for 30 minutes.

Next, make the chocolate shell by adding the cacao butter and honey to another heatproof bowl and place over the simmering water. Stir the cacao butter as it melts, then remove from the heat and mix in the cacao powder, peppermint and salt until completely smooth. Allow the chocolate to cool and come to room temperature for about 20 minutes. You do not want it to be hot while making the truffles.

Now it's time to assemble the truffles! Using a cookie scoop, scoop the peppermint filling into small balls, using your hands to flatten into round centers about ½ inch (1.2 cm) tall. Place the peppermint centers on the frozen baking sheet and place back in the freezer for 5 minutes.

Take the frozen baking sheet out of the freezer. Dip the peppermint centers in the chocolate shell and place back on the baking sheet so that the chocolate instantly hardens. Repeat this process until you have made all the truffles.

Place the truffles in the refrigerator for 5 minutes before serving.

REVERSE SEARED HERB
AND GARLIC CRUSTED BEEF TENDERLOIN

Nut Free, Dairy Free, No Added Sugar

Although the title may seem complicated, this tender, herb-crusted meat melts in your mouth, and I promise you will want to make this more than just once a year. The reverse searing method ensures that your meat is perfectly tender, juicy and has the best outer texture. Christmas can be an overwhelming time if you have food sensitivities or health issues, but this is great to serve because it is quite simple and everyone will enjoy!

SERVES 6

3 lb (1361 g) center-cut, trimmed beef tenderloin

1 tbsp (15 g) salt

½ tsp fresh cracked black pepper

4 large cloves garlic, crushed

1½ tsp (4 g) fresh thyme, finely chopped

1 tsp (3 g) fresh rosemary, finely chopped

3 tbsp (43 g) butter*

Prepared horseradish for serving, optional

*Use duck fat or olive oil for strict dairy free.

You want to prepare your meat a day ahead of desired serving time. Pat the meat dry with paper towels. Use butcher's twine to tie the meat off at 2 inch (5 cm) intervals. Season all sides with salt. Wrap the meat in foil and place in the refrigerator for 24 hours.

When you are ready to start cooking, remove the meat from the refrigerator and allow it to come to room temperature for 1 hour. Adjust your oven rack to the center position and preheat the oven to 225°F (107°C).

Place your tenderloin in a baking dish approximately the same size as the piece of meat.

Season all sides of the meat with the black pepper, garlic and fresh herbs, using your fingers to massage into the meat.

Bake the meat for approximately 1½ to 2 hours or until the internal temperature comes to 125°F (51°C). I recommend taking two temperature readings in different locations. Remove the meat from the oven and heat a large skillet with the butter for a good 5 minutes so that the skillet is evenly heated. During this time, your meat should still be rising in temperature.

Now sear the meat in the skillet for 4 to 8 minutes, rotating every 1 minute, or until the internal temperature comes to 135°F (57°C).

Place the meat on a cutting board and allow it to rest for 15 minutes before slicing and serving.

Serve with a side of horseradish if desired.

This & That

A center cut of beef tenderloin should have little to no fat on it. If you get a cut of tenderloin with some thicker sections of fat, trim them off prior to salting.

Be sure to trust the internal temperature of the meat rather than the suggested cooking times. As long as the meat comes to the correct temperature, I promise it will be delicious!

ROASTED GREEN BEANS
WITH CRISPY SHALLOTS AND CASHEWS

Dairy Free, No Added Sugar

My grandpa's all-time-favorite holiday side was green beans with cashews, heavy on the cashews, light on the greens! I have so many childhood memories of making these roasted green beans with my mom for our family get-togethers that they quickly became one of my favorites too! I like to use French-style beans, which are thin and have the best texture and flavor.

SERVES 4-6

1 pound (454 g) French-style green beans

2 shallots, thinly sliced

1 tbsp (15 ml) olive oil

2 large cloves garlic, crushed

½ tsp sea salt

¼ tsp black pepper

2 tbsp (29 g) butter or ghee*

½ cup (68 g) unsalted cashews

Use olive oil for strict dairy free.

Preheat the oven to 400°F (204°C).

Toss the green beans and shallots in olive oil, garlic, salt and pepper. Spread the beans evenly in a large baking dish. Slice the butter into small cubes and arrange throughout the pan.

Roast for 20 to 25 minutes, stirring halfway through, or until beans start to turn crispy. Stir in the cashews during the last 5 minutes of roasting.

BROWNED BUTTER WHIPPED CAULIFLOWER

Nut Free, No Added Sugar

Browned butter transforms your kitchen and plate into something magical. Not only does it smell delicious, but it has a dreamy taste too!

SERVES 3-4

1 large head cauliflower

6 tbsp (86 g) butter or ghee

1 tbsp (9 g) fresh sage leaves, finely chopped

¼ cup (59 ml) heavy whipping cream or coconut cream

1 large clove garlic, crushed

1 tsp (5 g) salt

Bring a few inches of water to boil in the bottom of a pan. Slice the cauliflower into florets, removing and discarding the inner core. Add the cauliflower to a steamer basket and place over the boiling water. Place a lid on top.

Steam the cauliflower for 15 minutes or until tender to touch with a fork.

Meanwhile, make the browned butter by warming a small pan to medium heat for 5 minutes. Add the butter to the pan, allowing it to sizzle. Continue heating the butter until it is golden brown and starts to give off a nutty aroma. Sprinkle in the chopped sage and sauté briefly so the sage can turn slightly crispy.

Drain the cauliflower and place it in the bowl of a food processor. Add the cream, garlic, salt and browned butter with crispy sage. Blend until smooth.

Best served warm.

This & That

If you are serving this to a group, I would highly recommend doubling the recipe. It will go quickly! Just make sure to do it in batches so that you don't overfill your food processor.

APPLE DATE SPICE CAKE
WITH MAPLE CINNAMON GLAZE

Nut Free

Apples, cinnamon and maple are my favorite combinations, and this apple spice cake is simple to make and lovely for a festive dinner party. Bursting with rich, spiced flavor, a small slice will satisfy your sweet desires. Serve with a dollop of whipped cream, vanilla ice cream or just as a slice—this cake speaks for itself. And yes, whenever I make this, slices quickly disappear at breakfast, because why not eat cake for breakfast!

SERVES 12

Coconut oil for greasing Bundt pan

1 large Granny Smith apple, cored and peeled

8 Medjool dates, pitted

1 cup (100 g) coconut flour, sifted

1 tsp (4 g) baking soda

1½ tsp (4 g) ground cinnamon

½ tsp ground nutmeg

¼ tsp ground cloves

¼ tsp ground ginger

Pinch of salt

8 eggs

8 tbsp (115 g) butter, or ghee, melted

¾ cup (184 g) whole-fat plain yogurt or coconut yogurt

½ cup (68 g) unsweetened apple sauce

4 tbsp (59 ml) maple syrup

1 tsp (5 ml) fresh-squeezed lemon juice

1 tsp (5 ml) vanilla extract

Maple Cinnamon Glaze

4 tbsp (58 g) butter or ghee

3 tbsp (45 ml) maple syrup

1½ tsp (4 g) ground cinnamon

Preheat the oven to 350°F (176°C). Generously brush all sides of a 9½ inch (24 cm) Bundt cake pan with coconut oil.

Chop the apples and dates into small pieces about ¼-inch (6-mm) thick. Set aside.

In a mixing bowl, sift together all the dry ingredients. In a separate bowl, combine all wet ingredients, mixing with a hand mixer until completely smooth.

Add the dry ingredients to the wet batter and continue blending. Scrape down the sides of the bowl and briefly blend again. Fold in the apple and date pieces.

Pour the cake batter into the Bundt pan, smoothing out the top with a spatula.

Bake for 42 to 46 minutes or until a tester comes out clean. Allow the cake to cool in the Bundt pan for about 10 minutes.

While the cake is cooling, make the glaze by melting together the butter and maple syrup, in a small saucepan. Once the sauce begins to simmer, lightly simmer for 3 minutes. Stir in the cinnamon and set aside to cool.

Drizzle half the glaze on top of the cake while it is still in the pan.

Cool an additional 10 minutes, allowing the glaze to soak into the cake before inverting onto a serving platter.

Drizzle the remaining glaze on top of the cake, slice and serve!

This & That

Coconut flour is very dense, requiring a significant amount of liquids to create a smooth cake batter. Do not be afraid to really mix your cake batter; this will help it rise and stay fluffy.

BUTTERLEAF SALAD WITH PROSCIUTTO SPIRALS AND CHAMPAGNE VINAIGRETTE

Nut Free, Dairy Free, No Added Sugar

Salty prosciutto spirals and tart grapefruit combine for a beautiful contrast of flavors and textures.
As a light side salad, this adds a pop of color and is a refreshing addition to your holiday feast.

SERVES 4-6

Champagne Vinaigrette

1 small shallot, minced

½ cup (118 ml) olive oil

¼ cup (59 ml) champagne vinegar

1 tbsp (14 ml) lemon juice

1 tbsp (15 ml) Dijon mustard

½ tsp salt

Fresh cracked black pepper, to taste

Salad Ingredients

2 heads butterleaf lettuce

1 avocado, sliced

1 grapefruit, peeled and sliced

3 oz (85 g) prosciutto

Whisk together all dressing ingredients and set aside.

In a large serving bowl, add the lettuce leaves followed by the avocado and grapefruit slices. Slice the prosciutto in half lengthwise and use your fingers to shape into small spirals, arranging throughout the salad.

Drizzle the desired amount of dressing on top, reserving any extras for later.

Toss and serve.

This & That

The dressing can be made a few days in advance. If you are doing a lot of entertaining over the holidays, I usually double or triple the dressing recipe to keep on hand.

When adding the grapefruit, be sure to set aside most of the grapefruit juice—otherwise your salad will become soggy.

POMEGRANATE MIMOSA SPARKLERS

Nut Free, Dairy Free, No Added Sugar

Sometimes life just calls for a glass of champagne, and I truly believe in celebrating!
These mimosas are very festive and sweetened entirely with fresh juices. If you do not want to have the champagne, simply top these drinks off with bubbly water instead.

SERVES 1

1 oz (30 ml) fresh-squeezed orange juice

1 oz (30 ml) fresh, sugar-free pomegranate juice

Champagne or sparkling water to top

Pomegranate seeds and fresh mint, to garnish

Add the juices to a champagne flute. Top with champagne or sparkling water, depending on preference. Garnish with pomegranate seeds and mint.

This & That

I typically use Champagne Brut because it is a dryer, less sweet champagne that pairs nicely with the sweetness of the juices.

CARAMELIZED ONION, SAUSAGE AND BACON FRITTATA TO SHARE

Nut Free, Dairy Free, No Added Sugar

The Christmas season usually means extra faces of family and friends fill the kitchen table, and this frittata is a great way to feed a hungry crowd. I usually prepare the sausage filling the night before so that all you have to do is assemble and bake. Full of flavor with each bite, this egg frittata allows the oven to do most of the work while you sip on Pomegranate Mimosas (page 236), catch up with family or open presents.

SERVES 6-10

1 lb (454 g) pork breakfast sausage

½ lb (227 g) bacon

1 small red onion, thinly sliced

12 eggs

½ cup (118 ml) coconut milk or grass-fed heavy cream

½ tsp salt

2 cups (272 g) fresh spinach

Preheat the oven to 350°F (176°C) and warm two skillets to medium-low heat.

Add the sausage to one skillet and the bacon to the other. Brown and crumble the sausage into small pieces and cook the bacon, until both meats are fully cooked.

Remove the bacon from the pan and set aside. Drain all but one tablespoon (15 ml) of the bacon grease and add the onions. Sauté the onions, stirring occasionally, for 20 minutes or until they are very soft.

While the sausage and onions are cooking, crumble the bacon into small pieces and set aside. Whisk together the eggs, milk and salt until frothy. I usually use a hand mixer because it helps make them light and fluffy when baked.

Add the spinach to the pan with the onions and sauté just until the spinach is wilted.

Add the sausage crumbles to the bottom of a 9 by 13 inch (22.8 by 33 cm) pan, then the bacon crumbles and finally the onion mixture on top. Pour in the egg batter. Tent the pan with a piece of foil.

Bake for 30 minutes, remove the foil and continue baking for an additional 5 minutes or until the middle is set, watching carefully at the end so that the frittata does not burn or dry out.

Slice and serve.

This & That

If you can tolerate dairy and love cheese as much as I do, sprinkle a bit of shredded Gruyère or cheddar on top before baking.

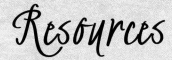

Resources

Tools Specific to This Book

Unbleached Parchment Paper

A grain-free baker's best friend. I always keep a few rolls on hand because it makes life so much easier! It is a brown or white paper, free of chemicals, that will not have your cookies and pie crusts ending in disaster. I like to use it when roasting potatoes or vegetables because it makes for a quick cleanup. I prefer the brand Beyond Gourmet, which is available at most stores or on Amazon.com.

Meat Thermometer

Every cooking environment is different—the cut of meat or heat of the day can drastically influence the result, which is why it is important to take the internal temperature of the meat. For recipes where this is particularly important, such as tender ribs and brisket, I have provided the end temperature results. The best cooking advice I can give you is to trust the internal temperature, not the suggested cooking times.

Smoker

You will notice a good amount of meats in this book cooked by smoking—a method combining heat from a natural fire and the firewood emitting smoke for flavor. The texture and flavor simply melt in your mouth, and you will soon be wanting to smoke everything! I used a natural firewood style of smoking to test these recipes. Yes, you can use an electric or propane smoker, but I cannot promise the texture and flavor will be the same. However, no matter what style of smoker you have, if you maintain heat and maintain smoke, you will have good results. Smoking meat can be difficult at first, until you really learn your own cooking environment and tools. Trust me, these recipes took a lot of time to develop and still need to be adjusted based on the cut of meat and even the weather conditions of the day. For smoking meat, here is the best advice:

First, go low and slow. Work to maintain a stable temperature, usually about 225°F (107°C), and constantly tend to the fire, adding fuel when necessary. Minimize the time that the lid is open to prevent heat from escaping. Like the old saying goes, "When you're lookin', you ain't cookin'."

Second, trust the internal temperature of the meat. If the meat does not come to the right temperature, it will not be tender. For example, yes, a brisket is safe to eat around 170°F (76°C), however it will not start to tenderize until 190°F (87°C).

Grain-Free Baking

When working with grain-free flours, it is very, very important to carefully measure the desired amount. Being just a little off can greatly alter your result. For the best results, I highly recommend sifting your flours before measuring.

Coconut Flour, Flakes and Milk

Coconut flour is my favorite flour to use, although it can be a bit difficult at times. Made from dried coconut meal, this flour is a great alternative for those who are allergic to nuts, and I find that with the right combination of liquids, coconut-flour baked goods are very light. Coconut flour is very high in fiber and protein, so a little goes a long way, usually accompanied by a lot of liquids. Coconut flakes are unsweetened and dried finely shredded coconut that I use for making crusts or mixing into granola. For the recipes in this book, I recommend using Let's Do Organic finely shredded macaroon coconut flakes for the best results. Coconut milk is a creamy dairy-free alternative that is used quite frequently in baking. I only recommend using canned coconut milk that is full-fat and unsweetened.

Nuts and Nut Flour

The most popular of the nut flours is blanched almond flour, which can re-create almost anything from pancakes to cookies, from cupcakes to pizza crust. Blanched almond flour is commonly available, however, I chose to use it very sparingly in this book. I wanted to offer some creative recipes using a combination of flours and nuts so that your tastes are always excited. My favorite nut to bake with is cashew because it gives a light and buttery taste—cashew pieces can easily be made into flour by grinding them in the food processor. When baking with nuts, make sure to use raw nuts that do not contain added bad-quality oils or salt. You will also notice the chestnut flour in quite a few recipes. This is an Italian flour made from ground chestnuts that has a rich, spiced flavor to it.

Psyllium Husk Powder

Psyllium husk powder is an indigestible fiber that helps bind ingredients together, making your gluten-free baked goods less crumbly. It allows my Nut-Free Sandwich Bread (page 30) to come together beautifully. Not to be confused with whole psyllium husks, the powder is finely ground and greatly contributes to the texture of your baked goods. You can find psyllium husk powder at most health food stores in the vitamin section or easily online. If you cannot find the powder, you can grind your own with a coffee grinder, however it may change the results slightly.

Arrowroot Flour and Sweet Potato or Potato Starch

Because grain-free flours are free of gluten and low in starch, baking can sometimes be very difficult, leading to results that either look like a brick or instantly crumble. Enter the safe starches such as arrowroot, made from the roots of the arrowroot plant, and sweet potato starch, made from dried sweet potatoes. Please note that sweet potato starch is much different from orange sweet potato flour and cannot be substituted (however, you can substitute potato starch). Sweet potato starch can be found online or at most Asian grocery stores. These white, flavorless starches are essential to the consistency of your baked goods or helping sauces thicken, however they are higher in carbohydrates, so if you are diabetic like me or working to overcome health issues, I recommend using them sparingly.

Tapioca flour is similar to arrowroot, but it is more difficult to digest for many people, including myself, which is why I chose to avoid it.

Unrefined Sea Salt

Unrefined salt contains important trace minerals that not only help keep your body balanced and hydrated but also support thyroid and adrenal function as well as build healthy bones. Selina Naturally's Celtic Sea Salt is my favorite brand of salt and the one I heartily recommend using. Their salt is completely natural, harvested straight from the ocean, dried at low temperatures and unbleached, which maintains its impressive nutritional benefits and taste.

I used exclusively Celtic Sea Salt when testing these recipes, so if you are using a different type of salt, I recommend adjusting the amount to your taste. But trust me, the flavor Celtic Sea Salt brings to your dishes is simply irreplaceable!

Sugar, Spice & Everything Not So Nice

With each of the sweet treats in this book, you will notice a lot of fat and protein, such as butter, eggs, whipped cream, nuts or coconut, in the ingredient list. When you eat something higher in sugar or carbohydrates, it is important to combine that food with a fat or protein. This slows the rate at which the sugars are absorbed into your body, keeping your blood sugar stable. So go ahead and add an extra pat of butter, ghee or coconut oil to your roasted sweet potatoes or slice of coffee cake and a dollop of whipped cream to your dessert!

You will notice the sweets, treats and desserts in this book are made with minimal sweeteners. They are still perfectly delightful, but I chose to limit the sugar quantity as much as possible. I did this because as a Type 1 diabetic, I wanted to create desserts that can still be enjoyed but will leave you feeling satisfied in the end, instead of making you sleepy or putting you in a sugar high.

In fact, your taste buds change over time, growing accustomed to the foods you eat. So as you start to eat less sugar, slowly your body will no longer crave sugar as it did once before. I absolutely love sweets, but I don't really crave them any more and would much rather have something savory, such as the Crackling Pork Belly Croutons (page 86) or Crispy Cheese Crackers (page 194) for a treat.

Sugar sneaks its way into just about everything—from breakfast sausage to dairy-free milks, from condiments to salad dressings. A seemingly healthy salad can be the worst option on the menu if the dressing is filled with sugar. So when in doubt, just double-check the ingredient list or make your own. Take a few minutes every week to prepare your staples, such as Balsamic Basil Vinaigrette (page 74), Homemade Ranch (page 168) or Chorizo Sausage (page 20). Keeping your kitchen stocked with healthy options is really the key to success!

A Guide to Sweeteners

RAW HONEY AND MAPLE SYRUP

You are probably very familiar with these common sweeteners, recognizing the honeybee or the little bottle that usually accompanies your plate of pancakes or waffles. Both raw honey and maple syrup have great nutritional benefits, but as with any sweetener, I recommend using sparingly. When selecting honey, it is important to choose raw honey that has not been heated, treated or pasteurized, because these processes destroy its valuable minerals, enzymes and antioxidants. It is important to choose pure maple syrup. Often pancake syrups you find in the store are combined with other ingredients such as corn syrup and chemical flavorings.

COCONUT SUGAR

Made from the sap of the coconut palm tree and dried to form brown crystals, coconut sugar is a great low-glycemic sugar. Coconut sugar will slightly change the color of your baked goods, giving off a brown tint, which is why I use it sparingly in this book. It is a great alternative to regular sugar with your morning cup of coffee.

My favorite of the sweeteners, maple sugar's texture is probably most similar to granulated cane sugar and really contributes to the consistency of your baked goods. It is probably the sweetest of the sugars I use, but the flavor is simply irreplaceable. Maple sugar gives your baked goods a rich flavor, and your kitchen will come alive with the dreamiest aroma. Substituting coconut sugar when a recipe calls for maple sugar will result in a different sweetness factor, color and texture, so I don't recommend substituting.

Cooking and Pantry Essentials

Grocery Shopping Cheat Sheet

The key to success with this way of eating is keeping healthy options available. When going to the grocery store, create a menu, make a list and shop the perimeter of the store. Choose real, fresh foods when possible. For packaged foods, when in doubt, take a quick look at the ingredient list. If you cannot pronounce the ingredients, it probably is not a good option.

FATS

» grass-fed butter or ghee

» olive, coconut, macadamia, sesame or avocado oil

» duck fat, beef tallow or lard

» palm shortening

» avocados

» full-fat and unsweetend coconut milk, from a can

» raw or grass-fed cheeses

» dried coconut or raw nuts

PROTEIN

» grass-fed beef, bison or lamb

» pasture-raised chicken or pork

» free-range duck or turkey

» cage-free, organic or pasture-raised eggs

» wild-caught fish or shellfish

» sausages, bacon or cured meats*

*Try to avoid added sugars, preservatives or MSG.

FRESH FRUITS AND VEGETABLES

» Try to choose organic, pesticide-free, GMO-free and seasonal options when available.

PANTRY ITEMS

» Celtic Sea Salt

» dried and fresh herbs and spices

» full-fat and unsweetened canned coconut milk

» nuts, nut butters or nut flours

» seeds or seed butters

» coconut flour or flakes

» dark chocolate bars (70 to 85 percent cacao)

» raw cacao powder, nibs or butter

» freeze-dried fruits

» unsweetened applesauce

» grass-fed gelatin

» olives

» coconut aminos

» vinegars

» tomato sauce, crushed tomatoes or tomato paste (look for organic and sugar-free options)

SAFE STARCHES

- beets
- squashes
- sweet potatoes or yams
- parsnips
- plantains
- potatoes
- pumpkin

SWEETENERS

- raw honey
- maple syrup or sugar
- coconut palm sugar
- molasses
- dates
- fresh fruits or freeze dried fruits

OTHER ITEMS

- fermented sauerkraut and pickles
- sparkling water
- kombucha
- coffee or tea

GRASS-FED OR PASTURE-RAISED MEATS

- US Wellness Meats
- Local farms, farmers markets or CSA groups

BACON, PEPPERONI OR HOT DOGS

- Applegate or US Wellness

WILD-CAUGHT FISH

- Vital Choice

GRASS-FED BUTTER OR CHEESE

- Kerrygold

EXTRA VIRGIN OLIVE OIL

- Kasandrinos Olive Oil

GHEE

- Pure Indian Foods
- Tin Star Foods

COCONUT OIL

- Tropical Traditions

GRAIN-FREE PASTA

- Cappello's

NUTS, FLOURS OR DRIED FRUIT

- Nuts.com
- Almond flour from Honeyville.com

GRASS-FED GELATIN

- Great Lakes Gelatin

KOMBUCHA

- GT's Kombucha
- Live Soda Kombucha

CHOCOLATE BARS

- Pure7 Chocolate
- Eating Evolved
- Nohmad Snack Co
- Righteously Raw

Acknowledgments

To Stephen, my husband and best friend: Thank you for daily living out this journey with me. Thank you for supporting me in every aspect of my life and encouraging me to complete this cookbook project! Thank you for surprising me with a new camera, taking me out to dinner when I was completely exhausted, letting me dance around the kitchen in a burst of giggles and wrapping me in your arms when I needed to cry. Some of my favorite memories with you will forever be written in these pages—perfecting the ribs and chocolate chip cookies—and I could not have written this book without you. When you are out to sea for long periods of time, I will hold tight to the memories we have shared cooking and creating together. You light up my world, and I love you more than I can ever express in words.

To Amber Schoniwitz: I truly could not have done this book without you! You are one of the most talented and kindhearted people I know, and I am so thankful you are willing to share your God-given talents with others. From the start, you believed in my vision for the cover photography and worked endless hours to make it come true. I will be sad when I move away from Hawaii and weekly dinners will have to stop, but I know we will be lifelong friends!

To my Mom and Dad: Thank you for never giving up on me and for encouraging me every step of the way. Thank you for instilling in me the spirit of perseverance, entrepreneurship and living life to the fullest. Thank you for your prayers over my life and health and for sending boxes of healthy snacks to my college when I was initially diagnosed. Mom, thank you for daily family dinners at the kitchen table growing up, something I didn't understand as a child but am so thankful for today!

To my sister: Thank you for sharing my obsessions for butter, cappuccinos and colorful tulips. Thank you for lying in the emergency bed with me the night I was diagnosed with diabetes and always being a loyal sister and friend.

To my many friends, family and recipe testers: I wish I could thank each and every one of you personally, but thank you for the texts, phone calls, emails and comments on social media encouraging me throughout this cookbook process. Many of your comments made me cry tears of joy and gave me the confidence to share these recipes.

To Kim Schuette: Thank you for encouraging me to become a NTP and helping me through the days of my diabetes diagnosis. Thank you for not only helping me professionally but also being a friend and a mentor.

To Karen Beyer: Thank you for being a loyal friend no matter where I move to across this country. Thank you for recipe testing and most important, your weekly encouraging texts and phone calls and always praying for me!

To my cover photography team—Katelyn Riechers, Annette Gomez, Loren Burgess, Laura Johnson, Vocabulary Boutique, Mimi and Lu Jewelry, Marisol Garcia Makeup and so many other people: Thank you for helping make my dream a reality and working countless hours on my behalf. I can never thank all of you enough for giving your time and energy from your hearts.

To the Page Street team: Thank you for giving me the chance to share my story and recipes with the world. Thank you for being patient with me on all the countless details and working to achieve my vision for this project!

To my blog readers and fellow Type 1 diabetes friends: Thank you for letting me share a piece of my life adventure and kitchen escapades with you all. Thank you for listening to my story and sharing your stories with me. No matter what health issue is thrown at you, never give up, and always make the effort to choose joy despite the circumstances. This book is written for you all, and I hope it inspires you to find joy in eating and life around the table.

About the Author

Caroline Potter is a Nutritional Therapy Practitioner (NTP) certified by the Nutritional Therapy Association and author of the blog Colorful Eats. After being diagnosed with Type 1 diabetes in college, Caroline radically changed her diet and developed a passion for nutrition, creating and sharing recipes and food photography. Caroline is completely self-trained and says that when you wake up each morning passionate about what you do, it makes life so much better!

Caroline started her business at the age of 23 with the idea that if her recipes and nutritional advice could change just one person's life, then the hard work would be worth it all. Despite living with a life-altering autoimmune disease, Caroline is thankful for diabetes, because it has shaped her passions and given her a platform for sharing her story with others. She works with clients all over the country, helping them with personalized nutrition plans and encouraging healthy eating habits, specifically with Type 1 diabetics. Her motto is "choose joy" despite what situation life gives you, because in the end it is always worth it!

Caroline believes that steak, hamburgers and butter are their own food groups and absolutely loves good cheeses and hot cappuccinos. As much as she loves traveling, swimming in the ocean in the afternoon and exploring the beautiful world around, she also loves curling up on the couch with her husband for movie night.

Caroline currently lives in Pearl Harbor, Hawaii, where her husband, Stephen, serves in the United States Navy. They love to cook together on the weekends and take their golden retriever, Libby, to the beach. Caroline says a good day is when ribs are in the smoker and friends are on their way over.

INDEX